D0041556

HANGING AND RATTLING

HANGING AND RATTLING

an autobiography of

W. E. "Ed" James

as told to

Dulcimer Nielsen

The CAXTON PRINTERS, Ltd.
Caldwell, Idaho 83605
1979

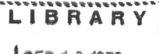

LIBRARY

SEP 1 8 1979

UNIVERSITY OF THE PACIFIC

368081

Western
Americans
F
746
J35

© 1979 BY
DULCIMER NIELSEN

All rights reserved

Library of Congress Cataloging in Publication Data

James, Ed, 1894–
   Hanging and rattling.

   1. James, Ed, 1894– 2. Idaho — Biography.
3. Idaho — Social life and customs. I. Nielsen,
Dulcimer. II. Title.
F746.J35   979.6'03'0924 [B]   77–78213
ISBN 0–87004–264–5

Lithographed and bound in the United States of America by
The CAXTON PRINTERS, Ltd.
Caldwell, Idaho
131088

To all Ed's "awfulsprings," and his many real friends.

Acknowledgment

My sincere gratitude goes to Ed, for sharing the experiences herein; to his daughter, Althaea Miettumen for her assistance and interest; and to my husband, Thor, who encouraged the writing of this book by saying: "Do it!"

Some Well Known Brands in Idaho Country

HORSE IRONS

Cougar Track — Ed James

Horseshoe Bar — Bill Brown

Bar Wrench — Jack Morris

Crow Foot — Granny Miles

T 5 — A. Carson

Heart — McLauflen

Circle Dot — Owner unknown

Quarter Circle or Sciver — on mare bought from Howard Lewis.

Flying V — Wild Horse Aperson

Flying W — Les Curtis

7 Anchor — Dean Husten

One Bar One — George Dixon

Seventy One — Sess Dixon (no relation to George)

Link — Ike Mills

Ninety Six — from Harney County

COW IRONS

"N" — Dean Husten

H L — Hugh Lister

Two F — Avery Scogens

Double O — Hanley Bros.

Dog Iron — Bruce Gray

Half Circle E — Howard Elkins

Z X — Biggest cattle outfit in eastern Oregon.

Hanging H — Dewey Moore

M B — Myer & Brown

Pine Tree — Hugh Night

Circle C — Charley Campbell, biggest cattle outfit in Idaho.

A running iron

Table of Contents

Introduction

"Live every day of your life and get all the kick out of it you can, as long as you don't hurt anyone else."

Born on Christmas day, 1895, Ed James has seen the country from six-guns to satellites, from mustangs to moon rovers, yet he has never lost his perspective, his integrity, or his good, common horse sense. He has the uncanny ability to see through the complexities of today's world to what is real and honest, and in the eight years I have known him, I have learned more about life and living than I ever learned from any other person. He has taught me what it is like to have — and to be — a real friend.

For a number of years Ed and I lived about three miles apart, each running small horse ranches in Grants Pass, Oregon. In fact I met Ed through horses — he was selling and I was buying. Horses are so much a part of Ed's life it is hard to think of one without the other. The man is an absolute magician with horses. He can knock a cantankerous thousand-pound horse to its knees, or gentle a tiny frightened foal; he can call a horse out of a herd by name and it will come to him and follow him like a dog without a rope or a rein. His horses understand every word he says to them. He says its his "gentle" voice — he always hollers at them as if he were mad, but they are never afraid of him. They respect and mind him though, and he never lets one get the idea it can do anything else.

What Ed doesn't know about doctoring livestock is hardly worth knowing, and I have known vets to ask for his help. I know he has saved me and many others a small fortune in vet bills over the years, and the only thanks he would accept was maybe an occasional jug of whiskey.

There came a time in my life when I was running my

ranch alone, and the work was getting me down, though I was too stubborn and proud to admit it or ask for help. One day I was out in the barn shoveling manure and the work was, quite frankly, damn near killing me. Then the horses started whinnying, and I saw Ed coming down the driveway on one of his "wobble-gaited" Walking Horses.

"Howdy," he said, as he tied his horse up at the hitching rail. He didn't say "Do you need some help?" or "Let me know if there's anything I can do."

He grabbed the shovel away from me, grumbled something about how a woman shouldn't be doing that kind of work, and spent about eight hours cleaning that huge old barn out. He was in his seventies then — I was about thirty — but he could and still can out-work me and several men my age all day long. He knew I'd been down in the dumps, and he not only helped me get caught up on my work, he had thought to stash a flask of whiskey in his saddle bags! A friend in need, and a friend indeed!

Many is the time when I would find myself alone at home on a rainy day with a touch a cabin fever. Then I would call Ed up and ask him how he was doing.

"Just hanging and rattling, as they used to say of a fellow on the high desert when he put up a poor ride," he'd reply. He meant he wasn't doing much of anything, either. "You'd better come over, Girl. I've got a jug here that's growing whiskers, and I hate to drink alone."

So I'd drive over — or if the weather wasn't too bad I'd ride — and Ed would meet me at the door with a big grin and a hug. He always made me feel like the most important person in his life, and although his house was not much more than an old shack, he always kept a warm fire going in the stove, and I always felt more welcome than in a palace. Quite often other friends and neighbors would drop in, and Ed made them feel like visiting royalty, too. I guess that's part of his magic. He makes his friends feel special, and he takes time to care. And he always keeps his word.

He'd break out a bottle and make drinks. No one can ever accuse him of being stingy. He always says once you break the seal, its an unwritten law that you throw the cork away. He mixes drinks that could easily tranquilize a full-grown horse, and many is the time I drove home from his place when I shouldn't have been on the road.

I can't resist telling one on Ed: One time when he'd ridden over to my place and we'd had a few drinks, Ed was feeling "about like a fellow always oughta feel." He got ready to go home, and of course he had taken the bridle off and tied the horse with a rope around its neck. Well, he untied the rope, climbed on his horse and started down the driveway. I let him get about halfway before I yelled after him that he might want to put the bridle on! Its fortunate that all his horses are so gentle, for all he had to do was holler "whoa" and the horse stopped and waited for him to put the bridle on. I still kid him about trying to ride home with no bridle.

On these rainy-day visits we would sit around for hours "peddling wa-hi" as Ed called it — an old Indian phrase for shooting the bull. Ed has a real talent for story-telling, and more than once I've heard others say, "Ed, you ought to write a book." I decided to practice what Ed has taught me: don't just talk about something; do it.

So pick a lazy rainy day, pour yourself a drink, pull up your favorite chair and join us for some wa-hi in the wickiup.

HANGING AND RATTLING

CHAPTER 1

Road Lizzards and Wagon Tramps

Not much happened before I was twelve. I used to do some high diving off the pier at Long Beach, California. I did miles of swimming, and sometimes speared sharks and stingrays. I never knew a mother; she died when I was too young to remember her. She was Cherokee, Dutch and English. My dad was Welsh, French-Canadian and Delaware Indian. So me, I must be just a mongrel. There were seven kids in our family: four girls and three boys. Ethyl was the oldest, and she was pretty much a stranger to the rest of us. Next was Ivadell, who raised the last three of us. Then Hazel, Steve, Gorden, myself, and a little sister named Madalene who died when she was only five. So I was really the youngest, the biggest nuisance, and always more or less in the way.

Early in the spring of my twelfth year Dad got itchy feet and wanted to go to Oregon. Hazel and her husband Joe, Ivadell and her husband Bill, Gorden and Dad rigged up three covered wagons. Bill was a old-time horse trader, Joe was an expert electrician, and Dad was a little bit of everything. He was not really an expert at anything except landscaping and growing things. He sometimes even filled in for a preacher; he knew the Bible, sure, but he was no more religious than I am, and hardly that.

We left Pomona, California that spring. I had gotten partly through the sixth grade, and there ended my school days. We of course had workhorses, saddle horses, and a lot of mixed loose horses. It was my job to make them follow the wagons. I had visions of a lot of horse chasing, but in a few days, after we got into strange country, I couldn't have kept them from following the wagons and only had to watch the new ones. Bill was always trading some trash horse for a good one, and usually made a few dollars to boot.

Bill was Irish, and Joe was German, and they didn't always get along. Bill could speak Spanish, and Joe couldn't understand a word. Bill never lost a chance to speak Spanish just to give Joe a hard time. Joe always said he was telling lies about him.

We were called "wagon tramps" or "road lizzards." Times were not good, and jobs were scarce. The year was 1907. We worked at anything we could find, stopping whenever one of us landed a job. It was just hard luck for any stray California pig or chicken. We ate whatever we could catch. At one place we were picking hops, and I met a little girl whose folks were wagon tramps, too. I liked her a lot, in a kid's way. I remember she was an especially nice kid, but she had so much hair on her arms, legs, and neck that I could hardly see her skin. I always wondered if she was that way all over. Some of the others made fun of her, but I was not big enough to do anything about it except get mad, and that of course was what they wanted.

We moved north, and at Burney I caught the first trout I had ever seen. I also saw my first porcupine — a female that had just given birth to a little one. It was still wet, and the quills were soft. I was fascinated by it, and played with the baby for awhile, until its quills started to dry and stiffen. It was such a big baby in comparison to its mother that I really wondered how she ever gave birth to it.

The next stop was Fall River Mills. I can remember that the volcano of Mount Lassen was smoking quite a bit. Bill got a contract building a road, and went into the construction and freighting business. All the work was done with horses. He and Ivadell lived there the rest of their lives. My brother Gorden stayed with them. (Gorden was exactly two years my senior; we were both born on Christmas day.) He eventually became manager of the general merchandise store there. Joe and Hazel moved on to Portland, Oregon, where he continued his trade as an electrician.

Dad and I took a light wagon that two horses could pull easily, and went to Oregon. Klamath Falls was our destination, but we landed in Grants Pass first. Dad said there was too much timber to clear in that country, so we hit the trail east through the Cascades. The road over Green Springs was the toughest road I ever was on. It was steep and rocky, with sections where someone had taken a sledgehammer, knocked out the worst of the solid rock, and called it a road. It was hard on the horses, and even harder on our old beat up wagon. But we made it to Klamath Falls, and from there traveled east to the high desert around Burns, near Harney and Malheur Lakes. It was an endless land of gray sagebrush, coyotes in bunches, jackrabbits by the thousands, wild horses and antelope everywhere. There were golden eagles, bald eagles, magpies, ground owls and ravens. Many of them are gone now. Poison was scattered from planes, and traps were built, baited with poisoned alfalfa and the wild horse was nearly exterminated. They tell me that they used every low-down inhumane method imaginable to kill and starve animals; but that was long after my time in that country.

The killing of Pete French was fresh in people's minds when we came to the high desert. The story has changed down through the years, but here it is as I heard it then: Pete French was a cattle baron, a cocky little man only five feet, one inch tall, but he proclaimed himself king of thousands of acres in that area. He hated the homesteaders who were moving onto what he considered his land. He would cause his cattle to break in and trample their little patches of rye grass, and if the homesteader kicked up a fuss Pete would uncoil his bullwhip, which was twenty-two feet long with a loaded butt. Many homesteaders were scared off their land until one of them stood up to Pete and shot and killed him in 1897.

Dad said the desert was too dry, so we turned back toward the Cascades. At the Narrows, between Harney and Malheur Lakes, a rancher was butchering and gave us a quarter of a beef. At that time it was okay to kill any fat beef you came across, if you needed meat, as long as you used it yourself. It was considered rustling if you tried to sell it, though. I noticed the beef that was given to us didn't have the rancher's own brand on it.

We moved north to Prineville and traveled up the Crooked River. Dad finally located a 160-acre homestead just north of Alkali Flat, and we began to grub and dig and drag sagebrush and rocks off the land. It looked like a lifetime job, but Dad was a hard worker. We worked from the time we could see in the morning until it was too dark to see at night.

All went well until Dad started telling me that if he didn't have to build and clear a farm, he would go back and spend the rest of his life with Ivadell. Well, I got more than I could take of it. One night, when some neighbors invited us over for supper, I made some excuse to send Dad on ahead, saying I'd come later. It was early in October, I was coming fourteen years old, and when next I saw him, I had World War I, a wife and three kids behind me. I still consider this to have been one of the very best moves of my life.

I hit for the high desert, and that night I laid out on the ground and about froze. That desert can get cold at night. I killed a young jackrabbit the next morning, and broiled it over a sage fire. That is, I burnt it on the outside and it was raw inside, but I added a little salt that I had thought to bring along and made a meal of it. Then I started on, east and south.

CHAPTER 2

Charley Couch and the Horseshoe Bar Buckaroos

I was afoot with one quilt and little else. I finally came to Held, a little post office about forty miles southeast of Prineville. I asked if there were any riders in the country, and an old lady told me that Charley Couch and the Horseshoe Bar buckaroos were at the Rawhide corrals, and told me how to get there. I hit the trail and got in just as they were scattering to eat. Couch told me to grab a plate and help myself, which was always customary in that country in those days. He told me to stay the night, and rustled me up some more quilts and a tarp, then they all went out to work the wild horses. I wasn't asked where I had come from or where I was going.

Next morning I helped Mrs. Couch gather sage firewood, and did whatever chores I could help with. While we worked I told her my troubles.

That evening Charley took me off to one side and said, "My wife told me about you, and while I don't think much of picking up stray kids, you had better stick around and help Mrs. Couch with the chores, as you did this morning."

I only stayed a few years.

I probably would have died from hunger and exposure if I hadn't run into Charley Couch, as I was headed away from all civilization, and I would never have gone back. I had left Dad a note saying I would not be back, and now he could go back to Ivadell and live. I heard afterwards that he stayed the next day, then hit the road for Fall Rivers Mills and Ivadell.

That evening some of the buckaroos showed me how to make my bed on half of the tarp, and pull the other half over the blankets with about three feet to spare. That way when it rained I could pull the spare tarp over my head, as well as my saddle and gear. I learned to pick a high spot of ground to sleep on, and in heavy rain to dig a ditch around my bed unless you had a stand in with the cook and could sleep under the chuck wagon.

In the morning, long before daylight, Charley dragged the blankets off me and told me, "Rattle your hocks! Day will soon bust, and we're late already."

I had only pulled off my boots, so it did not take me long to get to the fire, some coffee, biscuits and leftover meat. I found out later that we usually had hotcakes, fried meat and coffee, but that morning they were late. There was a heavy frost on the ground, and I stood shivering by the fire. The darkest, coldest time of night is that time just before dawn.

Mrs. Couch, or Nell as everyone called her, told me, "Stay around the fire and watch and keep out of the way until the riders are gone."

The saddle horses were in the corral, and I could hear the fellows yelling and laughing and cussing, and the horses running and bawling, but it was too dark to see a thing. Then I heard someone holler "Open 'er up." I could hear horses going in all directions, some of them trying to unload their riders. One came toward the fire, then bucked off out of sight, with a rider right behind him on a horse that was behaving, herding the bucking horse and rider in the direction of that day's ride. Of course I found all this very exciting.

Nell told me, "This happens every morning. At times they buck right through the fire, bedrolls and all. Everyone has to look out for himself." This early morning rodeo was with broke saddle horses. I soon learned the wild ones put on the real show.

The best way to get warm was to get busy, so I went to work helping Nell with the pots and pans. About 1:00 P.M. she gave me a pan of potatoes to peel, and she started a meal, saying the buckaroos would probably be back in a few hours. They showed up about 3:00 P.M. with a bunch of wild horses, leaving a long, low dust cloud behind them. The wild horses were put in one corral, and the saddle horses in another. The boys pulled the rigging off their hot, sweaty horses, kicked off their chaps, then washed up at a bench lined with wash pans and pails of water. They dried off at the fire, then grabbed tin plates and cups and helped themselves to meat, beans, fried potatoes and coffee. This was the main meal of the day.

They sat around talking and laughing and kidding each other about events of the day. Then they went back to the corral to work out the wild bunch. The best ropers saddled big heavy horses, with which to rope the wild horses for branding and gelding. Others built a fire just outside the corral for heating the branding irons. A few wild horses were let into the working corral, and one was roped and thrown to the ground. One man jumped on its neck, caught its lower jaw and one ear, and doubled its head back on its neck so it couldn't get up. Others tied its feet, and it was branded, and if necessary, gelded.

I stood outside the corral taking it all in, helping to keep the fire going and the irons hot. The fire was called the "kitchen" and the irons had to be red hot. They were used not only for branding but also to sear the arteries on horses that were gelded. The whole scene was one of dust, men running and horses falling; hard, dirty, fast work, and not without some danger. It was all part of a "mare chaser's," or horse buckaroo's, day. I decided there and then that I wanted to be a horse buckaroo.

Most of the horses that had been branded were turned back on the range, but about fifteen were held back to be ridden, to keep the riders in practice, and also, it seemed, just for the kick they got out of it. But it was a necessity too, for they had to be able to ride mean, fighting horses. The roper caught a chosen horse by both front feet, threw it and someone held it down while others worked a saddle and halter on it; they let it up just as a rider jumped into the saddle. Then it was man against horse. The others all sat on top of the corral and cheered for both the horse and the rider. It was fun for the rider, if he didn't get thrown, and fun for all the rest whether he stayed or not. After they had all ridden — or tried to ride — the rest of the wild bunch was turned out on the range, and the fellows came back to camp. It was the end of another day for the mare chasers, and they relaxed with some coffee, and some of them rolled cigarettes with brown paper and Bull Durham or Duke's Mixture tobacco.

It was then that Charley said to me "Come on, kid. Its time we had a pow-wow."

He asked about my life and family, and whether I had run off. I told him the whole story.

When I had finished he said. "I can tell you have told me straight, and that's always best. If you hadn't, you could have stayed another night and then hit the trail. Don't blame your dad. No one ever really knows another's life, and it makes a fellow feel better if he can think the best of others. Remember your dad left you the whole United States to make a living in. This is a hard life. There's no such thing as working hours, or Sundays off, and no one your age. If you stay with us it will be hard work. Most of these fellows are the salt of the earth, but some are just no good. Most of them will play tricks on you, and you won't always think they're funny. But stand up under it and you will find others will take your part. Take a joke even when its tough, but stand up for yourself when you know you should. These riders are young, and they don't miss a chance to get a kick out of whatever they are doing. You will not know which are real men under the hide until something turns up to prove them. Some of them are just like you — just did not have a home and grew up amongst a hard outfit, as you will do if you stay. You will find most of them are good men, but they won't take dirt from anyone, and will fight at a word, with guns if necessary. Those that won't just don't last long on the high desert and don't belong here.

"Try to stay out of trouble and do your best at your job, for your own pride and the respect of others. We will rustle you up some kind of an outfit, and I'll see to it you learn what is expected of you. Remember, not as your boss, but as your friend, try to do a little more and a little better than is expected of you. You will earn every cent that you get. We need a 'rango (wrangler) to herd and protect our saddle horses. Right now its being done turn-about by the regular riders, but I need them on the ride. So you see, I do need you. I'll pay you $30 a month plus your grub, and you've got the whole high desert to sleep in. You can stay and help around camp, rest up and get a little meat on your bones and then decide. Its up to you whether you want to stay."

I said, "I don't need any time to decide. I'm ready to go to work, and I figure I'm plumb lucky to land the job, and I will earn every cent you pay me."

"That's talking like a man!" Charley held out his hand. "Shake on it. Your pay started this morning. We will go put your time on the books. By the way, what's your name?"

I told him my first name, and he said, "Hell, I can't remember that and couldn't pronounce it anyway. What's your middle name?"

I told him it was a lot worse. He asked me to spell it, and I said, "I'm not sure I can, but it starts with an 'E'."

"Good enough! We'll put it down as Ed James. The boys will no doubt call you Jesse, but don't let it bother you. Most of them have about forgotten their real names, and its probably a good thing for them."

We started back toward the fire, and I turned to him and said that I appreciated what he was doing for me and I wanted to thank him.

"I know what you mean," he said quietly, "but out here we just don't thank anybody. If we appreciate something we try to show it sooner or later by returning the favor.

So for awhile I helped Nell with chores around the camp. They soon rode out that part of the range and we moved. We just piled everything on top of the chuck wagon, and a couple of riders trailed the saddle stock behind. Usually each rider had a string of nine saddle horses. There were about a dozen heavy roping horses, and four work-horses on the chuck wagon, which Nell drove. We moved about twenty miles and camped at the Stockade Corrals. These had been built by digging trenches, standing whole juniper trees up in them and tying the tops together with rawhide. The corrals had been built many years before and were still in good shape, as juniper will last for ages.

A morning came when one of the buckaroos didn't go on the regular ride, but stayed and drank coffee and talked to me and Nell until well after daylight. His name was Bob — he was usually called "Old Bob," as he was the oldest rider on the job. He must have been nearly thirty, and was all stove up from having horses fall with him. Nell told me he had broken both legs, and was busted up from many injuries, but although he was no good on the ground, seldom talked, and seemed to live just to ride, he was still one of the best ropers and mare chasers in the outfit.

He rustled around and found a saddle for me; "an old hull" he called it. It was a slick fork (no swell at the forks), with a high cantle, and the rigging was on the outside. They sure didn't waste any leather on building it, but it was strong and in good shape, what there was of it. He got a new saddle blanket, a stout headstall and spade bit, an old pair of chaps, a grass rope and a pair of spurs.

"There ain't an extra gun," Bob told me.

Nell said, "I've got one, if you think he will run onto someone to shoot the first day out."

We packed our outfits up to the corral. He threw his saddle on the ground with the horn down, sort of on its side, gave it a yank as he dropped it and the cinch, shirts and stirrups were all lying smoothly on one side. I dropped mine with the horn up and all the rigging underneath.

Bob pulled off his hat and shook his head. "Well, maybe I did the same thing when I was a kid. Let me show you how to lay a saddle down. You don't want your riggin' all curled up, 'cause sometimes you just don't have time to straighten it out when you get on. Besides, once the leather curls up it never does straighten out plumb again."

We went into the corral where Bob roped a sorrel horse. He showed me how to use a horsehair rope for leading or tying my horse. He called this rope a "McCarty" (actually "mecate," a Mexican word). He tied it around the horse's neck and down through the hackamore. I led the horse out and started to climb on, but Bob stopped me and showed me how to double the mecate and put the loop end down my chap leg. When a horse fell or I got unloaded, the loop would come out and I would have a chance to grab it and maybe save myself a long hike if my horse got away. Bob roped and saddled his own horse, then told me to ride to one side of the gate. He leaned down from his horse and swung the gate wide open. The saddle stock came out of the corral in a bunch, heading for a ridge a mile away. Some were galloping, but most were trotting as Bob and I galloped on ahead, leading them to the ridge. There Bob stopped them and we sat for a few minutes until they were settled down and grazing.

"Come on," Bob said, and I started to follow behind him. "Ride up beside me! Hell, kid, do you want folks to think we are a couple of dudes, Injuns, or sheepherders?"

We got to the ridge top and there was nothing in sight but a small herd of antelope. They had not seen or been hunted by white men enough to be afraid of us, and they just watched us awhile, then walked off in the other direction.

Bob began to teach me a 'rango's duties. "You always want to look around, because there might be a wild bunch of horses over the next ridge. They have to be chased off. If a wild stud gets too close he will try to drive your horses into his bunch. Sometimes you even have to shoot a wild stud to keep him from fighting your saddle horse or stealing your "cavy" (his word for saddle bunch). Once you lose your cavy to a wild bunch, its almost impossible to get them all back. A tame horse gone wild will, within a week, be the wildest of the bunch and the hardest to ever corral."

We rode back to the cavy, and they were grazing quietly. I noticed a few of them with horseshoes tied in their forelocks and of course asked the reason.

"Those horses have not been caught for long. They are liable to try to get away if they see a wild bunch, but as soon as they start to gallop that horseshoe hits them on the head, forcing them to slow down, so the 'rango can get around and chase them back."

We just sat around until I spotted a long, low dust cloud way off to the east.

Bob said, "It's always a good idea to get between the cavy and any dust you see. It could be a wild stud and his bunch, and a 'rango has to turn them away not short of a half a mile from the cavy, or you'll be in trouble."

Soon we saw that it was a wild bunch, led by an old broomtailed mare. Then a couple of the backaroos showed up over a low ridge from the south, and they turned the bunch north, up a draw and into the wing of the corral. More riders materialized from behind the wild horses, crowding them on up the draw and into the corral. Bob explained to me that the corrals were always built uphill from the entrance, or wings, of the corral, as horses will tend to stay in a bunch running uphill, whereas downhill they tend to split up. The wings are two long fences fanning out from the corral, serving to funnel the wild horses into the corral. Sometimes the wings were made of burlap, with the ends hidden in brush or rocks. The corral was sometimes just built of brush piled high. A wild horse won't jump if the walls look solid and he can't see over the top. Sometimes there will be a troublemaker in a bunch that will try to go any way but into the corral, and he will usually take several horses with him. These troublemakers more often than not had saddle marks on them — tame horses gone wild. When one of them was caught, the buckaroos branded it and cut its tail off, and turned it back to the wild. Whenever one of these "stub-tails" was spotted, he was allowed to escape as soon as possible.

We moved the cavy back to the corral, and joined the rest of the riders for the "royal gorge," as they called their main meal of the day.

Next day, if you could call it day — the stars were still blinking and they looked as big as coffee cups — the riders were already gone, except for the one who was to help me that day. They called him "Brutal Bert," because he was always threatening his saddle horse, telling it he would cripple it if it didn't "look a little out," though he never got around to carrying out his threats. That day went pretty much as before, only we had to scare off a wild bunch the first thing; but they were really wild, so it was easy to do. About the middle of the morning a single three-year-old stud showed up and we ran him off.

Bert told me, "Run off any good looking stud, but if he's a pin-eared scrub, the best thing you can do is feed him to the coyotes."

But to me, they all looked good, prancing back and forth on a ridge with their heads and tails high, snorting and whistling a high, piercing whinny you could hear for miles.

Each day a different rider would be my helper and they

all kept me busy lassoing clumps of sagebrush, to practice my roping. After about a week, Charley took me out to the corral, picked out a horse for me, and said, "Saddle up kid, from now on its up to you. The only time you'll have help is when quite a few horses are added to the cavy, then you'll need help holding them together for a few days until they get acquainted. Here is Nell's gun and belt. Don't use it unless you have to."

I had no trouble at all that first day alone, and was both disappointed and glad; but mostly glad, as I was only a kid, and to tell the truth, a little scared. After the ride a couple of the riders helped me corral the cavy, and Charley asked me how I'd made out. I told him okay. He looked at me, then turned and walked off without saying anymore. I knew I had done my job right. Charley didn't waste any words, although he was always ready to listen. I learned that the fellow who ran off at the mouth soon had no one around to listen to him.

We wore simple clothes. In the summer, boots, cotton socks, overalls and jumpers, or vests, hats and scarves. They were not like the scarves they wear in movies now, but long silk scarves, a foot wide and long enough to wrap around your neck with both ends hanging down your back to the top of your cantle. We had leather chaps, some shotgun style, some with wings, and in the winter we added cotton work shirts and chaps made out of mohair (angora goat hide). These chaps never got wet, the long hair shed the rain well. While riding, our guns were strapped to the forks of our saddles. On foot we wore them on our hip or leg. You couldn't chase wild horses all bundled up with heavy coats and gloves, but we were all young and had good circulation, so we stayed fairly warm as long as we were moving around, except when a "norther" was blowing. Then it really got cold.

One rider, Old Carson, told me, "You've got to be tough. If you can't chew Five Brother's tobacco, ride into a blizzard, spit straight into the wind and not close your eyes, you're not tough and don't belong on the desert no-how!"

It was not quite that bad, but we really suffered at times.

The horses we rode were high-withered, long-legged, fast walkers. High withers gave you something to hang a saddle on. A saddle will slip off a round-bellied, smooth-backed horse, like some of today's fat quarter horses. And long-legged, fast walkers got you where you wanted to go without jog-trotting. Its bad enough to eat dust on a long ride, without being on some short-gaited, jog-trotting horse that shakes your guts out. The saddles we used were double rigged (two cinches) both wide, with the back cinch loose until you wanted to rope something; then you tightened both cinches. When you got the job done you loosened the front cinch so it was easy on the horse, and as they used to say, "let the back cinch flop, so long as the horse doesn't get his leg through it." These flank straps, or rear cinches of narrow leather made today would cut a horse in two if you roped something big and hard to hold. They came into existence with the dudes and the low-cantled saddles.

Along about the first of November Nell left us, as she did late every fall, and an old homesteader took her place as cook. Pickins was his name, but everyone called him Slim — unless they were sore at him and called him something they thought was more appropriate. That never jarred him. He claimed the smartest mare chaser was lucky if he had anything better than sagebrush for brains. He was a good cook, and everybody liked him, most of the time.

Charley encouraged me to use my rope, but to lay off roping any horses unless I had help getting my rope loose. I found out it was a real disgrace to lose your rope. You could get bucked off or your horse could step in a badger hole, and fall and get away from you — that sometimes happened to the best — but to lose your rope was just too bad for you.

Our first trip into town was quite an event for me. Burns was small then, with just one dirt road down the center, and hitching rails, or poles, the full length of both sides of the street. As we rode into town, the buckaroos began roping signs and barber poles, and I asked Red McCullen what was going on. Without answering, he roped a barber pole and took his turn dragging it up and down the street, in general raising dust and hell. Everyone got a big kick out of this, and even though their fun was known to get a little rough at times, the town's people seemed glad to see us. It took awhile to get all our horses quieted down and tied to the hitch rail. Most of the horses had never seen a town, and were plumb scared of someone on foot.

Charley gathered us all together and said, "Before you blow all your money, I want you to come with me."

We went into a saddle shop and Charley told me to give him all my money, except for $5. Then all the fellows chipped in and they bought me a complete riding outfit — even some of them I had figured didn't like me as they had treated me pretty rough at times — they all chipped in and most of them bought me extra rigging besides. This included a new gun and belt of my own. Of course I hurried to the back of the store and got into my new outfit. I just shed my old rigging and left it lying on the floor, and I walked out, rather stiff, but plenty proud! Wasn't I a Horseshoe Bar rider, and wasn't that the top outfit on the range, or anywhere else? No one mentioned that I was just a 'rango.

Charley told me not to load my new gun or put any bullets in the belt. "Stay with me. If the boys get to drinking and things get a little rough you and I will rattle our hocks out of here. We don't want you getting plugged. I can always get another rider, but I need you. I want to see you winter with us, and we will need you more than ever come spring. That's when we catch the real wild horses!"

I don't suppose I would have seen spring if it hadn't been for Charley riding herd on me. But he never gave the idea then that he was really taking care of me.

The next morning most of the riders showed up, but some I never saw again. Nell had told me that usually happened — everyone said "howdy," but no one ever said "good-bye."

Winter wore on, and it seemed that I was half frozen most of the time. I rode out with the regular riders now and then, for the saddle stock was cut way down. They were fed mainly on oats or rolled barley, and learned to eat a lot of grain without foundering. There wasn't much else for them to eat, but they would paw the snow off and eat some of the black sage that was left. It took a good winter horse to last three years. If they didn't get crippled in hidden rocks or badger holes, they got burned out eating so much grain. The saddle horses were tall, rangy stock, as gaunt as greyhounds, and tough. No horse was ever brushed or curried. If they were dirty or sweaty we took a sage branch and scraped off the worst dirt just around where the saddle went. We figured nature put the dirt there to protect them from cold in the winter. In spring they lost the long hair and other accumulated covering.

Finally spring came, and I knew that I was one year older. I hadn't known when Christmas (my birthday) had come — one day was the same as another, and most of the time we didn't even know what month it was. When you commenced to feel warm and your horses started to shed off their winter coats, you knew it was coming spring, and you were glad of it. No more shooting poor horses that were too weak or too old and sick to get up anymore. No more shooting colts whose mothers were dead. I got to hate snow, and each new snow storm. It always meant shooting something to put it out of its misery.

With the coming of spring, Charley told me: "We won't need a 'rango for awhile. I'm going to make a mare chaser out of you. This time of year we get the really fine wild horses. They are weak from winter and our saddle horses are hard and grain fed. You will get $35 a month."

I graduated from a grass rope to a riata, made of rawhide. Most riders carried not less than fifty feet of rope. Mine was thirty-five feet long, a hand-me-down that was a leftover from another rider's broken rope. Unlucky for the fellow who broke it, but lucky for me, as even at that time it cost $1 a foot to have a riata made. Some riders carried as much as seventy feet, but thirty-five was all I could handle.

We began to get some good wild stock. We'd rope one, choke it down, halter it and tie it to a juniper tree. When we were ready to take it back to the corrals, we'd put a riata around its neck, down through the halter ring, then get on our own horse and fight it out. After a wild horse pulled back and choked itself down a couple of times it found out it could not get away, and it was surprising how fast they learned to lead on a slack rope.

Now and then, when a particularly nice wild horse came in, the fellows would keep it and break it to use for their own saddle stock.

One day Charley said, "Catch one for Ed."

They caught a three-year-old bay mare, threw her and put my saddle on her. As they let up, I lit astraddle of her, and never did get my foot in the other stirrup. I didn't ride her, I just hovered over the top of her, hanging and rattling for three or four jumps, then landed all over myself in the middle of the corral. Charley told me I did pretty well for the first time, and of course the whole bunch of riders started telling me what I did wrong and what I should have done.

Red McCullen said, "We are starting Jess all wrong. You get him so he can ride a little three year old, then put him on gradually tougher horses, and maybe if he doesn't get his neck broke along the line he will be a bronc twister. You ought to start him out on the meanest, toughest old stud first, and when Jess can keep company with him, the rest will be easy!"

Charley told Red to go to hell, and by then the little bay was rested up, and they threw her down again, and looped a quirt over the horn. They told me this time to lean back and stay with her, and if I could, to grab the quirt and knock the filling out of her, but whatever I did, leave that saddle horn alone. They promised me they would beat hell out of me if I ever tried to hang onto that "convenience knob." (Besides, a bad horse would jerk you apart if you hung onto the horn.) Charley told me they would spread-eagle me and hold me down, and that he would personally flog me with a chap leg. I still believe they would have done it. But I knew it was no disgrace to get bucked off, and as they told me, I could only break my neck once, so I jumped on again. (As the saying goes, "There never was a bronc that couldn't be rode, and there never was a rider that couldn't be throwed.") I got a better start this time, grabbed the quirt and rode the mare until she quit. One of the riders rode up beside me and pulled me off. No one said much, they just went on with their work. I heard one say, "That filly wasn't much to ride." Another said, "That kid got the hang of it. He will ride someday."

So I graduated from lowly 'rango to full-fledged buck-aroo. I was the youngest rider in the outfit, and proud of it, so I tried just that much harder to be a top hand. I gradually began to ride older horses and consequently I got bucked off more often. Two of the riders took special interest in me: Red McCullen and Howard Elkins. Red was the best rider I ever knew, and Howard was the best roper, so I had the finest teachers, and they swore they would make a top hand out of me, or kill me.

When I tried to ride a horse that was a bit too much for me, Red would hit me across the back with his riata and tell me, "Straighten up and ride, or I will beat hell out of you!"

I was more scared of Red than of any horse, so I stayed on horses I never could have ridden otherwise. Some of the "hobble-stirrup" riders tried to get Red to hobble my stirrups on the tougher broncs, but Red said, "Jess will ride straight up, fan his bronc and keep his right hand in the air, or I'll kill him. You hobble-stirrup riders are a disgrace to a clean rider, and you belong over across the Cascades with the rest of the wed-footed riders."

A hobble-stirrup rider had rings on the insides of his stirrups, and ran a strap between these rings under the horse, pulling it tight. This way they could ride anything that could stand up. We considered it cheating.

The riders encouraged me, saying Red was teaching me proper, and I was doing okay with my riding. But as a roper, Howard said I couldn't hit the ground with my hat.

"Keep at it; you've got to get the twine to go where you want it. Hell, there ain't always goin' to be someone around to rope your horse for you! How can you hold down a job if you can't rope your own horse? Or are you going to be a sheepherder?"

Those were shooting words on the high desert in those days, and if I had been older I probably would have just cussed him. Instead, I felt like going out in the sage to bawl. Charley happened to overhear, and later took me aside and talked to me.

"Howard was only getting after you for your own good. Listen to him, and keep practicing. He can out-rope Red, but Red can out-ride Howard any day. And look at me, I'm considered a number-one, all-around hand, but I can't claim to be in Red's class. I never saw anyone take the hard knocks and get laughed at as much as you have, but you've kept on trying, and that's what it takes. You may never be as good at riding as Red, or at roping as Howard, but if you don't get your neck broken, you will beat heck out of some of these red-tailed buzzards who are making fun of you now. Now, damn it, go on back and don't let anyone get you down. If they get too rank, tell them where to get off. But as I said, listen to Red and Howard. They may be tough on you at times, but they are both all for you under their hides."

We corralled at a place called Guana Valley, where the wild horses had been chased before, and would run if we got within a mile of them. You could always tell an old stud that had been chased before. He wouldn't gallop between you and his bunch; instead he would just sort of bounce back and forth on all four feet, head and tail high, stopping now and then to whistle and snort. A wild killer stud would usually trot back and forth, then whirl to face you with his head just off the ground and his ears laid flat on his neck. We usually shot fighters unless they were exceptionally fine animals. The ones we did catch were hard to subdue. Sometimes two men on horseback would rope a stud from opposite sides. With two taut ropes pulling against each other, the wild stud couldn't get at either rider, and he soon quit fighting. Once we corralled him, we'd draw cards to see who got to ride him.

On the first morning after we'd camped at Guana Valley, we jumped a wild bunch before the sun had come up. I was on the south side of the bunch when they split up in some rimrocks. It was my job to stay with them, and to bring them back if at all possible. These horses acted as if they were headed for California and knew the trail! I tried to turn them back, but there were some fast horses in the bunch, and no young colts to slow them down. About all I could do was gradually work around them and get ahead. Wild horses always have a certain range, and I knew that in time they would swing back on their own. But the day was getting late, and I was miles from where I'd started. This was an unusually good bunch, about twenty head, led by a bay mare and bossed by a gray stud. Every time I got the herd turned the way I wanted them to go, that gray would get

between me and the bay mare and turn them away again. I
finally got them headed toward Guana Valley and decided
to call it a day.

The evening star came out, and it looked as big as a
saucer. The wild bunch was about a quarter of a mile ahead
of me when I quit chasing them and they settled down for
the night. I tied my horse to a juniper tree and waited for
the stud to come back to see what had happened to me, as
they always do when you have chased them all day. He finally showed up, and walked back and forth on the ridge
until it got so dark I couldn't see him anymore.

I had to lay out that night, without food or blankets. I
have read stories about men who slept in their saddle blankets, but I never was tough enough to sleep in wet, sweaty
blankets, and while I may be hard-headed, using a saddle as
a pillow would cramp a dog.

Next morning I saddled my horse and walked him
around until it got light. He was only about half broke, and
when I got on, I had to double him around to keep him from
bucking. I knew he smelled the wild bunch, and he wanted
to run. As I topped the ridge I saw the wild bunch just pulling out, about a half a mile away, with the bay mare walking
in front, and the gray stud herding them from behind. When
he spotted me he whirled and challenged my horse with a
shrill whistle. I could just feel his urge to come back and
fight, but he did not quite have the nerve. As he stood there,
head and tail high, he was really a beautiful sight. Then he
evidently thought better of fighting, turned and trotted off
after the bunch. They were headed in the right direction,
and my horse settled into the long swinging trot that a
marechaser uses the most. It had been a cold, miserable
night, but as the sun came out I began to thaw, and everything was going my way so far. I began to watch the ridges,
as I knew it would not be long before some of the riders
would be coming to look for me.

I traveled about ten miles and the bunch had slowed to a
walk when suddenly the stud threw up his head and whistled, facing west. A rider showed up on the ridge, and the
old stud rounded up his bunch and pushed them into a gallop. The rider fired a shot, signaling the others that I had

been found, and soon three other riders joined us, and the chase was on. I rode behind, "on the drag," and two riders stayed on each side of the bunch. After a couple of miles they slowed to a trot, and about noon we were joined by some more riders with a second wild bunch. We pushed the two herds together and headed for the wings of the corral on a dead run. The wild horses poured into the corral, the gates were slammed shut, and I was more than ready to get on the outside of some grub.

My lying out the night before had not been unusual, it happened to all of us at times. Luck had been with me this time. That gray stud could have fought me, or lead his bunch into rough country and scattered them but the herd had turned in the right direction, and the riders showed up at the right time. Still, lying on the cold, hard ground at night, hungry and lonely, a rider sometimes wonders if there is not an easier way to make a living. But there is something about mare chasing and all that goes with it that a rider never gets tired of. To see the stars on a clear desert night, bigger and brighter than they are anywhere else; to hear the old studs whistle, and to watch them work their hearts out trying to keep their herds from danger; to hear a coyote howl in the middle of the day or to hear the night hawks swooping down out of the sky with their wings set, making a low whirring sound, or voicing their call which is unforgettable and beautiful — you really know that you are in wild, unspoiled country, and that you belong and are a part of it.

As I dropped off to sleep that night, I thought about that old gray stud out there in the corral with his bunch. The boys had told me that he had gotten away from them three times in the last three years, and they had intended to shoot him. Now I had brought him in. I sure felt that I had earned my $2 in the last forty-eight hours.

The next day I asked the ropers to haze the gray stud into the breaking corral. "I will see if I can keep company with him," I said.

Charley told me, "You must be plumb loco!"

"Charley," I said, "that stud and me are pals. Didn't we

run together all day, and camp together all night? He'd be downright disappointed if I let anyone else rough him out."

Charley shrugged. "Hell, its your funeral, and I hope he suns your moccasins. Maybe after this you'll use your head for something besides a hatrack."

They threw the old gray, held him down and saddled him. I pulled the halter rope up tight and told them to turn him loose. I jumped on as he came up, and from there we went bug-hunting. He bucked high and fast and crooked, but he didn't hit the ground too hard, and I managed to stay with him. Then he got to throwing himself into the corral, which is a good way to break a leg. One of the riders got between us and the fence, grabbed my halter rope and snubbed the stud up close. That stopped the bucking, and I climbed over the back of the rider's horse onto the ground.

The only thing Charley said was, "I'll bet you didn't learn nothing."

I gelded the gray the next day, and Red asked me if I wanted him for my string of saddle horses. I said yes, and Red took over to train him.

We went from Guana Valley over to Steen's Mountain, down past Malheur Lake, then north. There we hit some truly bad country, with high, rough hills and soil only inches deep — poor range, hard on both horses and riders.

As we got far to the north-east we could see the Idaho hills in the distance, and we began to run into a different type of horse. We called them, "shave-tails" — they had very little hair on their tails and manes, like mules. They were mostly red or blue roans with freckled noses and white around the eyes, and occasionally there was one with a white blanket. They were big, powerful horses. Rocks, brush, steep ground, holes or washes didn't bother them. The older ones were exceptionally mean and hard to handle.

We ran into Indians there, as we did all over the desert. They were always friendly, and always hungry. The squaws tried to sell moccasins and gloves made from well tanned buckskin, for twenty-five to thirty cents, depending on the size of your feet or hands. These Indians called the shave-tailed horses "Palouse cuiton" which meant: Palouse Indian horses. (Palouse Indians were an offshoot of the Nez Perce Indians.) Those old shave-tail studs seemed to be all mean, and they didn't fear a man on horseback. We had to kill several of them, but of course we all wanted a shave-tail for our string before we left that country. Charley grumbled that people would take us for a bunch of lousy redskins, but I am satisfied that we introduced some of the first Appaloosa blood to the high desert.

We worked our way south, and around the head of Crooked River we began to run into a lot of our Horseshoe Bar stock. Just outside of Shaniko I really made a killing for myself. I was alone, trying to spook horses out of the canyons, when I heard a lot of noise just around a bend. I was riding the gray horse I'd caught in Guana Valley. He started acting up, and when we rounded the bend, there was a black stud all tangled up in some brush and rocks. There was a riata around his neck, and the way the ground was torn up he'd been there a day or two. Most of the fight had gone out of him, and I was having more trouble with my own horse. The gray would never forget he had once been a wild stud — he was what we called a "stag." Stags made the best mare chasers. You could stop on a ridge and look the country over and not see a thing, but your old stag would look way in the distance and all of a sudden his ears would go forward and he would roll the rowl in his spade bit and paw the ground and he would take you straight to horses, maybe five miles away — far beyond your vision. Other times while trailing a wild bunch in broken country, if you lost sight of them, your stag would trail them at a long, fast trot, and take you to them by scent. Anyway, I finally got him quieted down enough so I could lean over and grab the black's riata. After a few half-hearted efforts to get away, the black gave up and led as if he was glad to be with us.

The black was a fine horse, a five year old, and I sold him to one of the riders for $75, which was a really big price at that time. The riata proved to be sixty feet long, and practically brand new.

Charley said, "I've had several horse thieves ride for me, but when one of my riders comes in with a stolen riata with a horse on the end of it, that's really stretching things, especially when there are no witnesses!"

I took a lot of kidding, but it had been a very lucky find. No doubt the owner of the riata heard about it, but he would be the last to claim it, as a buckaroo just never could live down losing his rope. No one ever did claim it.

I was riding down the Deschutes River, where the river cuts a canyon with high, rocky, roughly sloping sides, looking for a way to climb out on the east side. For once I was riding a gentle horse, and I was looking for any small bunch of wild horses to haze out for the rest of the riders to bunch up and corral and drift out of that part of the country. We were really off the Horseshoe Bar range, and most of the stock there were Indian ponies, not considered worth raising.

I spotted a thin blue ribbon of smoke about halfway up the rim, and I thought it was probably an Indian fire, as they build small fires. I knew it belonged to not more than one or two Indians, most likely one lone old buck. Most of the old bucks could talk some English and they could understand a lot if they wanted to. They usually had no use for white men, but I had enough Indian blood that I was accepted. I hoped maybe this would be an Indian that I knew, as he could tell me where the ponies ranged in there. I rode up on this old buck, and it happened that I knew him well. I knew most of the Indians on the Warm Springs Reservation, and at that time they were not allowed off the reservation without permission, for which they seldom asked and seldom received, but they sneaked off. I rode up to within thirty or forty feet of him, and knowing Indians, I didn't say anything for awhile. I got off and watched him. He was heating his little clay pipe on the fire, then pressing it on the calf of his leg around where he had cut the skin criss-cross. He had it pretty well burned all around, and he would grunt and mumble something in Indian each time he applied the pipe. Finally I thought I had waited long enough so that he would answer me. He was "Oh-Hi Ike," one of the oldest Indians on the reservation, and he hated the white man; that was mostly on his mind all the time.

I said, "Hi, Ike. Snake bitum?" and waited.

He finished burning his leg, then pressed all around the burn, grunted and finally said, "How Jess." He waited a couple of minutes, put his pipe away in a buckskin sack, sat there awhile, then said, "Them dam' snake son-of-a-bitch him no speakum, bite-um Injun go rock. Them dam' snake son-of-a-bitch!"

He did not seem to be bothered about being snake bitten, but was plumb put out and mad at that snake because it didn't rattle!

I asked him, "Where wickiup?"

"Juniper Springs." he answered.

I told him to get on my horse. He shook his head and said, "Buckaroo no walk. Injun walk."

Finally I got on my horse, kicked my boot out of the stirrup and told him to get up behind me, as the old buck could just barely drag his leg along. I had to all but lift him up behind my saddle. He didn't weigh much, as he was old and just a dried up buckskin sack of bones. I thought the burn was worse than the bite. We made our way up out of the canyon, and Juniper Springs was just over the next low ridge, down in the draw. When we got to the ridge, old Oh-Hi wanted to get off. I told him, "Stay on, I'll take you into camp."

He said, "No good. Injun more better get off walk."

I didn't think he could walk, and I asked, "How come Injun no ride?"

He said, "Yo no tellum Injun ride. Squaw laugh dam' squaw no good."

I told him that I would not tell. He said, "yo come wickiup all time eat yo all same skocum Injun, white man hide."

Those old Indians did not waste words, but you could depend on them if they liked you. If they didn't, they wouldn't talk.

We came to the head of Beaver Creek, a tributary of Crooked River, and camped with "Granny" Miles, a horseman who was raising Morgan-Appaloosa crossbreds. We rode that upper country out as far west as Wildcat Mountain. We didn't catch too many horses, and as we drifted back toward the high desert I almost got my everlasting at dry Paulina Lake. I was chasing two yearlings, which is the most brainless age of any horse. They pulled to my right; I tried to bend them further right, and my horse was giving me all he had. The sagebrush was high and dense. I was gaining a little, riding low on my horse's neck at a dead run, when he swung to the left so suddenly that he almost lost his footing and me, too. Through an opening in the sagebrush I saw a crater some thirty feet deep and a hundred feet across, peppered with big rocks which had sloughed off the rims: a sure death trap! One of the yearlings went in, and the other just missed it. The fall killed the first one, but I managed to rope the other one. I didn't get over that scare for some time, and after that, if I couldn't see ahead, I went wide of any dense sage.

I took the yearling in and gave him to old Granny Miles. The colt wasn't worth a punched nickel, but a mare chaser just doesn't let anything get away if he can help it. Granny put his Crowfoot brand on the left shoulder and was just as pleased as if I'd given him a good horse. He was so proud of his horses that he all but starved himself to keep from selling any of them. He always said he'd like to sell a few hundred, but if you picked one and tried to buy it he'd have some excuse why he didn't want to sell it.

It wasn't paying to ride in that area, so we went back of Maupin Butte. We corralled at the old Grindstone Ranch for a few days, and from there went into the table rock country. We began to strike more horses, which were quite wild and hard to handle, as they had been chased and shot at by the cattlemen who had infested that range. The cattlemen used a method known as "creasing" to catch wild horses. They shot the wild horse in the neck, between the cord, just below the mane and the spine. This stunned a horse long enough to tie it down. The trouble was, they killed about nine out of ten. It took a great deal of skill and luck with a rifle to hit a horse just right.

The weather was wet, and the mud was from a few inches to a foot deep, with rock underneath and slippery crevices in the rock. Sometimes your horse would break through the muddy soil and step into a crevice and fall end-over-end. If you were lucky the momentum would throw you beyond your horse. You always got skinned up and often broke bones; I have plenty of scars on my frame to prove it. It gets so it just chills you to have a horse fall. We hated that country and were glad to get back to the desert proper. Badger holes were bad enough, but every year the mud on those tablelands was sure to cripple some horses and riders. A few of the buckaroos are still out there, with no headstones, no one to sing over them but the coyotes, and usually no one knew from where they came or their real names.

We were camped a the Jaggi corrals on Camp Creek. There were a few wild bunches as well as mixed-brand stock around the Jaggi and Twelve Mile Tables. Near Twelve Mile we jumped a wild bunch, and I knew we were in for some hard riding. Everything went well until we started to make the run to force them down into Camp Creek. My horse was running low and level, giving me all he had, which was plenty, when he broke through a badger hole and went down hard! I sailed out ahead of him and my mecate pulled from my chap leg as it should. Grabbing it as I jumped up, I ran sideways to pull my horse off balance when he got up. He was still struggling to get his hind leg out of the hole. When he did get up, he was stifled and of course ruined for life.

Some of the riders held the wild bunch while Howard Elkins roped a wild mare, and another, Blizzard Smith, held her down. We worked my saddle on her, put a hackamore and mecate on her, and I straddled her when they let her up. She lit out running and bucking, but the boys got her headed in the direction that the wild bunch was going, and soon we were amongst them, all headed for the gap that led down into Camp Creek and the Jaggi corral. I was corralled with the wild bunch and crowded up against the fence where I climbed off. That was the only time I was corralled, but I helped corral some of the other riders the same way. I was lucky as the Jaggi Table has but a few junipers — not a bad country to run a horse on. The mare I was on stayed on her feet and the ride did not last long. Its impossible to guide a wild horse, they get so scared they will run into trees or over a bluff if they get near other riders. I would never make such a ride for the fun of it and I don't want to

do it again, but there was no help for it under those circumstances — we just did not walk if we could help it, even to
cross a street.

We got back to the desert and out of the mixed cattle
country. The beef had been a change of diet for us. Out on
the high desert we ate horsemeat, and we only butchered
two-year-old fillies. Even good beef can't beat that.

We moved on to Wagontire Mountain, then west to
China Hat, south through Devil's Garden and Fort Rock.
This was real wild horse country, and the western edge of
the Horseshoe Bar range. We went back to Burns, then on to
Buck Creek, the home ranch. It wasn't a ranch at all, and
today it would be called the headquarters. Bill Brown was
there. W. W. (Bill) Brown owned the Horseshoe Bar. At
Buck Creek he owned a good house and a store as well as
several so-called ranches all over the desert.

Bill always said, "I am morally certain that the store business just don't pay." (He was always "morally certain"
about one thing or another.)

The Horseshoe Bar brand was known everywhere in the
west. Bill paid taxes on up to ten thousand head of horses.
His real love, however, was for sheep. He didn't like horses,
and thought less of buckaroos, but he claimed he needed
the money from both to keep his sheep going. We didn't
think anymore of him than he did of us, and I guess we both
had reasons. Sheep just don't get along with other stock.

Bill used to stock up his store, put change in the cash
box, and take off with his bands of sheep for a month or so.
He'd nail a sign on the wall of his store with the prices of
everything, and when you went shopping you were your
own clerk. When he got back, Bill usually found the shelves
and the cash box empty. I guess he was right about the store
not paying.

If you went into Bill's camp and wanted money he
would tear off a label from a can, or use a piece of board, or
whatever material was handy, and write you a check. His
"checks" were always good. I have been told that a bank in
Prineville still has some of those checks.

I was in my third year with Charley and the Horseshoe
Bar buckaroos when I begin to get cramps in my legs.

They'd double up when I rolled out of bed, and it took two men to rub my legs until the cramps eased up. They got worse and came on more often. Charley said they were called bronco twister's cramps, and were caused by riding too many rough horses. He said the best thing for me to do was to quit riding and get a job punching cows for a few years. This was a letdown, as we mare chasers considered cowpunchers to be only a notch or two above sheepherders. My cramps got worse so I had no choice.

If the riders were real busy, the "bronco twister" roughed out all the mean horses. That was what he was paid for, and that is why I got cramps so badly — I was just too young to keep it up. A bronco twister got the top wages and he earned them. He was sometimes identified as "the buckaroo that rode the mean string." It was his job to take the kinks out of the really tough horses, and to teach them to stop, go, and double each way before the horse was turned over to the regular mare chasers. If there was lots of time, most any of them would tackle a mean horse — usually on a bet. Most of them had an idea that they could ride anything and they were all for proving it. They usually got their moccasins sunned and lost the bet, and everyone got a kick out of it.

CHAPTER 3

Cowpunching

Howard said he had had enough of mare chasing and suggested that we go over to Crooked River country where he knew some people. So we each took a good saddle horse and hit for cattle country.

We got to the "N" cattle ranch just out of Paulina. They were busy working cattle, so we sat and watched until the owner rode up and shook hands with Howard. Howard had ridden for him before. When I was introduced, the owner said he had heard of me, and knew that I could handle a knife (gelding) and keep company with a rough horse. Of course he knew Howard was good with a rope.

When he learned that we were looking for jobs, he said, "By dickies, what're you sitting on your horses for? Get your knife out, Ed, Howard get down your twine — we need you both in the corral."

Howard roped for a couple of hours and never missed a throw. It looked as though his riata was alive. He'd whirl it around, turn it loose, and it would crawl under a calf, which would jump right into the loop. That was really expert roping, especially since Howard hadn't worked with cattle for three years. In roping horses, the loop is thrown so it stands up on front of the horse's front feet; with cow critters its thrown so it lies flat on the ground in front of the calf's hind feet. I don't know why in the rodeos today they catch a cow critter by the head and drag it around until the team roper can catch it by the hind feet. In my day anyone who caught the head first was told to put up his rope.

I guess I did my job all right. Old By Dickies used not only a brand and ear-marks, but also cut a wattle on the calves' necks. (A *wattle* is cut in the hide this way: *ʃ* It heals up and draws together and hangs down like a loose finger. A *burr* is the same only on the nose. A dewlap is cut in the loose skin of the neck and *necktie dewlap* is cut at the top and bottom and attached in the middle: ᵃ .) It was kid's play compared to cutting and branding horses.

We got the cattle worked out and the owner said, "By dickies, I am glad you boys showed up! The spring ride is on, and I need you bad. I'll pay you $45 and grub, that's $5 more than the top hands get hereabouts."

It was a letdown in pay for both of us, but I just couldn't ride any mean horses for awhile, and Howard wanted to get out where he could be with people again. (During my time with the Horseshoe Bar I went a stretch of one year and three months when I never saw anyone but riders and an occasional homesteader.)

Howard was a good mixer and wanted to go to dances and such. I was sixteen then and had never been to a dance in my life. If a woman spoke to me I was ready to stampede. I didn't know what to say or how to act, and I felt as out of place as a jackrabbit in a pen full of coyotes.

Cowpunching was slow and dusty work. I missed the high desert and was homesick for the wild horses and the coyotes howling in the daytime. The ranges had fences here, and you came onto ranches or homesteaders' shacks every ten miles or so. But Howard told me I would soon get over it. Old By Dickies, whose real name was Dean Huston, had a wife and two daughters, and they seemed to understand how I felt. After I got over my initial awkwardness I enjoyed talking to them, and I began to think back to my life before I went to the high desert.

After the calf ride was over there was to be a dance, and of course everyone was to go. Half of me wanted to light out for the desert, but the other half was developing a crush on the boss's oldest daughter Velda. I went to the dance, scared though I was. The boss's family rode in a two-seated buggy, or surrey, and Howard and I and the other punchers rode behind on our saddle horses. Long before we got there, we could hear the tramping of feet, the fiddle playing, laughter and whoops, and we knew there was quite a party going on. We went in and found a room full of people. There were lots of kids, and they were having just as much fun as the adults, just dodging dancers or trying to dance themselves. It wasn't a large room, and everything had been cleared out for the dance except a wood stove for heat, and a few benches made from boards laid across low sawhorses.

Some of the cowpunchers began to tag men on the dance floor, as there weren't nearly enough women and girls to go around. Someone grabbed me, introduced me to everyone, and told me to get in there and take a girl away from one of the dancers. I got back in a corner out of the way and watched the fun. That was the first dance I had ever seen, except for when some Horseshoe Bar riders danced with some girl in a barroom to the music of a worn out phonograph. I wasn't about to slap one of those fellows on the back and ask to dance with his partner. Around midnight a woman came over and talked to me, and when the fiddler started again she said, "Come on!"

I hung back like a spooked colt, stammering, "I've never tried to dance, and I just don't know how."

She said, "You can't learn any younger, and you never will learn if you don't get out there and try. Everyone out there had to learn once." With that she grabbed me by the arm and dragged me out among the dancers, saying, "Just grab on to me, its really easy, and everyone else is busy trying to dance themselves."

I don't know how I ever got through it, but finally the fiddler stopped and we sat down on a bench. Soon another woman came and sat down on the other side of me and told the first woman to run along, that it was her turn to dance with me.

Then we had midnight supper in another room. It looked as if everyone had tried to bring a bigger box of grub than their neighbor. When we went back to dancing I noticed that they had put quilts down on the floor behind the stove, and most of the little kids were asleep there. The boss's daughter danced with me, and she helped me as much as she could by chasing off some of the fellows who wanted to dance with her, but finally I got tagged. I was going to go sit on the bench, but just then a couple danced by, the girl gave my arm a pull, and the fellow's back came around toward me. I was plumb scared, and I still don't know how I did it, but I touched him on the back and danced off with the girl.

Then I started to look around, and I noticed that lots of the others weren't doing any better than I was, and no one paid any attention to them. I began to relax and enjoy myself. We danced until daylight when some of the people began to gather up their kids and go home. We went back to the ranch and slept most of the day, did our chores and crawled back into bed.

After the calf roping season was over, it was time to put up hay. Howard ran buck rake, and I worked on the stacks. The boss was a good stacker, and he taught me a lot in a short time. It was one of the hardest jobs I ever tackled, really man-killing work, and the stacks had to be built just right, so they would shed the rain and melting snow.

We were sent over to Madras to pick up a bunch of cattle the boss had bought. On the way back, at the head of the North Fork of Crooked River a storm came in. Lightning started flashing, and thunder shook the air. You could smell the heat. Our saddle horses had little streaks of lightning curling up from their ears, and the cattle had the same thing from their ears and horns. Now and then lightning would hit a tree and crack like a rifle shot only louder. It was spooky, but we were mainly afraid that the cattle would stampede. There would be no stopping them in those second growth thickets, they would scatter from hell to breakfast. They milled around and bawled a lot, but we held them until the lightning passed. Then it opened up and rained. In no time we were wet to the skin; even our boots were full. That was one night when everyone was glad to see the first gray streak in the east.

We pushed the cattle as hard as we dared. You just don't let cattle trot if you can help it, the owners don't want any flesh knocked off them. So we kept them at a walk, which is an awfully slow and aggravating pace when you're wet and tired.

We got that bunch into the home ranch and were told that a neighboring cattleman, George Dixon, had "borrowed" us. He needed extra hands to go to Klamath Falls to bring home a herd of Mexican cattle he had bought. I never saw such stock before or since. They were every color but what good stock should be: spotted, red and blue roans, brindles, and some white and black roans with dark noses like Jerseys. They were small cattle with high withers and low behinds, and heads and horns straight out of a nightmare. They were all ready to fight. When we turned them out they headed north at a run, and it was some time before we could get them settled down. They traveled more like horses than cattle. There was just no way to make them walk, when we tried to hold them back they would shake their heads, roll their eyes, loll out their tongues and make at lunge at our horses. They had long, curved, sharp horns, and the horses were afraid of them. We moved at least three times as fast as we would have with native cattle, as a long, swinging trot seemed to be their natural gait.

When we delivered them, old By Dickies and George Dixon were both there. George was all grins, but Dickies just sat his horse, and finally pulled off his hat, turned to George and asked, "Why in hell did you ever buy such cattle?"

George said, "I got them cheap."

"Such cattle are too high at any price," By Dickies told him. "I hope you don't intend to turn any of those Mexican bulls loose on the range. If any one of my boys comes onto one of them, it won't stay a bull long, and I don't care if they cut them starting at their throats. The best thing you can do is trail the whole bunch to the Redman slaughterhouse. You might get some of your money back, and keep the friendship of your neighbors, too. I for one will not rope one of those bulls; I'll put a bullet in it first."

He turned his horse toward the barn, cussing to himself. George said he would move them in the morning. Of course the punchers got a big kick out of it. By Dickies told us that night that if we cut any of those bulls he hoped they would all bleed to death. We did cut several of them, but no doubt most of them lived. Those cattle did help a lot later on. Not as breeders, of course; they wouldn't improve a flock of sheep. But when they were turned loose on the range they soon scattered amongst the native cattle. One time a bunch of our cattle and some of the Mexicans ones were in some thick second growth brush, and old By Dickies was worried about how to get them out. Howard said it would be as easy as shooting salmon on a riffle, but I had my doubts, for I knew those Mexican cattle could sneak around in the underbrush like deer. Howard told me to go about a half a mile past him, then we would both roll big boulders down into the thickets and spook the cattle out. I had used rocks to spook out deer and bear, but I had never thought of doing it with cattle. Those Mexican cattle were just as wild as any deer. It worked, and our native stock stampeded out with them. When we trailed cattle the Mexican ones were always out front, helping to keep the herd moving, and we even took a few to market. In comparison they made our beef look better to the buyers.

We were working on a drift fence on the ridge between the Crooked River country and the John Day country. There was a dance Saturday night in Paulina, so we cached our tools and went to the dance. When we got back to the job, we found that someone had relieved us of our tools and a few spools of barbed wire. Howard was cussing when the boss rode up and asked what was wrong.

Howard told him, "Some s.o.b. either watched me cache the tools, or found them after we left camp. Anyway, they're gone."

The boss scratched his head. "I don't see why anyone with any brains would steal something to work with! But never mind. I saw a bunch of wild sorrel horses on Wildcat Mountain, and if you and Ed can take the time off, I want the young stallion in that bunch. I'll give you each an extra's month's pay, and you can have the rest of the bunch if you want them."

Of course we were more than glad to get away from cattle for while and chase horses, to say nothing of the extra pay. So Howard and I took off, and when we had ridden a few miles we came to a camp with three men. We happened to know them, and one of them had once ridden with the Horseshoe Bar. They were gathering anything they could corral. (In other words, they were horse thieves.) They told us that they had spotted the little band of sorrels with the stallion that the boss wanted, and that it would be a cinch for the five of us to corral them. They had plenty of food and bedding so we stayed with them that night, and the next morning we corraled the band with no trouble. There were thirteen horses in the bunch, all sorrels of one shade or another, all pretty fair stock, and all "slick," or unbranded, horses. We picked out the stallion for the boss and one each for ourselves, and told the other three boys they could have the rest. The man who had ridden with the Horseshoe Bar was called "Wild Horse," as that was all he seemed to live for. Years later, by coincidence, I met a man at Klamath Marsh with the same last name as "Wild Horse" and similar features. I asked him if he had heard of Wild Horse.

He said, "I ought to know him, he's my nephew. He lives near Bend, is married, has a family and raises cattle. He's not stealing horses anymore."

I said, "I didn't mention that part of his profession."

He grinned. "I could tell by your expression what you were thinking."

We both got a kick out of it, and there was no harm done. I have known several horse thieves that were good boys, and a few that were only good for buzzard feed.

We broke the three wild sorrels to lead, gelded the boss's horse, and went back to camp. Howard and I packed up our gear, and cached the extra grub where we knew the horse thieves would find it and hit for the home ranch. We stopped at the Five Horse Ranch, owned by "A" Carson, about ten miles below Paulina on the Crooked River. We stayed with "A" a few days and broke the sorrels. When we got back to the N Ranch, old By Dickies acted as if we'd brought him a gold mine. He named his horse Blondie. I'll always remember Blondie; he couldn't buck for nothing, but he piled me into the corral dust one day when he caught me off my guard. I should have been able to ride him with both feet out of the stirrups, but those things happen once in awhile.

We rode the upper Beaver Creek, down to the Grindstone Ranch, then south to Maupin Butte. There were no ranches or corrals there, and as far as I know we had the last real open range round-up there. We gathered about 2,000 head of cattle, with cattlemen and cowpunchers from all over the state of Oregon representing lots of different outfits.

In those days of open range, stock often "drifted" a long way from home. That was part of what roundups were all about — to brand each year's new calves, gather up the cattle that belonged to each outfit and drift them back toward home range. I remember one Hereford bull from the "OO" (Double-O) Ranch that belonged to the Hanley Brothers near Burns. That bull had drifted a long way, and no doubt he had had some help, as he was a top animal. I know for a fact that OO bull had stayed with the stock at Maupin Butte, and although that wasn't considered crooked, it wasn't doing the OO Ranch any favor.

We surrounded that big bunch of cattle, and ropers would pick out cows with calves, rope the calves, and brand them with their mother's brands. If they didn't have the stamp iron, they used running irons. Some of the fellows were real artists with running irons, even though they were technically illegal.

Howard and I fed cattle that winter using bobsleds and jackson forks. The next spring we decided to go to Idaho. It was Howard's idea because his mother lived there. It made no difference to me, and it was a good reason to see some new range. I had about seventy-five head of horses on the Jaggi Table, and we decided to gather up the best of them, plus whatever slicks we could catch that were worth taking, and hit the trail for new country.

At Dagos Lake all the wild horses came from miles around to drink. They would run out into the lake up to their bellies and drink until they looked like they would burst. When we spotted one we wanted we would chase it on our horses. They would only run about a half a mile, then their tails would fly up, their heads would droop down and we could ride right up and drop a rope on them. They were so full of water that they had no fight left in them. It never seemed to have any bad effects on them.

We kept the horses we were gathering on some pasture I rented. There was an outbreak of rabies in that area, so bunching our stock together was taking some risk, but there was no help for it, as we wanted to get a bunch to take to Idaho. One horse I was riding got to grabbing at any brush that touched him, and I noticed he was more headstrong than usual, and was frothing at the mouth. I broke off a branch and touched him on the side of the nose. He grabbed it and his teeth popped viciously. I knew I was on a rabid horse. He had to be shot, but if I got off, I risked being bitten. So I pulled my gun out of the scabbard, got him stopped, kicked my feet out of the stirrups and pulled the trigger. As he went down I jumped clear. He fell with his back to me, dead. Luckily, I was only about three miles from camp. I hung my saddle in a tree, letting it swing clear so that the porcupines couldn't get at it. (They will chew up leather.) I was lucky again, as Howard was in camp and heard my shot. He brought an extra horse to pick up my rigging.

The next day I went down to see "A " Carson, and found him madder than a red-tailed buzzard. Horse thieves had stolen two horses out of his barn a week before, and he had turned it in to By Dickies, who was a deputy sheriff. By Dickies had gotten a few men together and ridden around, but had no luck. "A" told me that we were going to the dance in Paulina that night. He said he needed me, so of course I went. After the midnight supper, everyone was about to start dancing again when "A" stepped out to the middle of the floor and held up his hand. He was well known as one of the squarest and toughest men in the country.

He said, "Sorry to interrupt your fun, folks. I won't take but a minute. Two of my saddle horses were stolen a week ago, and with due respect to our deputy sheriff and his posse, they haven't been found yet." He paused a moment. "If Dutch and Spider ain't in the barn by daylight, me and Jess are going out and get the coyotes who stole them. Much obliged, folks, go on with your fun."

Before daylight the next morning I took a lantern out to the barn, and in the first two stalls were Dutch and Spider munching hay. I hurried back to the house and told "A".

All he said was, "Jess, I knowed they would be there." He went on fixing breakfast and never brought up the subject again.

CHAPTER 4

The Back Country of Idaho

Howard and I chased horses for a few more days, then we went into Paulina where Howard received a telegram from his stepdad, Dick Green, saying that his mother wasn't expected to live long, to come at once. We rode one more day, then hit the trail. We tied our horses head-to-tail, alternating gentle ones with wild ones. There weren't enough gentle ones to go around, so the last two wild ones were tied together — a gray filly of mine and a two-year-old bay of Howard's. We kept these two in the corral until the rest of the string was moving in the right direction, and as soon as I let them out, they took off for the dim distance. When I caught up with them they had straddled a juniper bush and gone down, breaking the filly's neck. Of course the bay colt was still tied to her. I cut him loose, and he was so confused he just ran back to the bunch and stayed there.

We went past Burns and east to the Gap Ranch. We had no more trouble until we got to Boise. We were trying to keep to the outskirts of town when we came to a sign in the road saying "No Loose Stock Allowed." Howard said we would try to sneak through, but we did not get far before Howard turned and motioned me to go back. We turned the bunch around and headed for the hills at a run. We got off the road and onto the hillside when a car with red lights all over it pulled up. Someone got out and hollered at us to stop.

Howard yelled back, "To hell with you. We are out of your rotten burg!"

We kept on going. The hills were high with nothing growing on them. Just one bald hill after another. In a couple of days we came to the Boise River and followed a road upstream to a bridge at the mouth of Rattlesnake Creek. We crossed the river and went up the creek to the Green Ranch.

We didn't get there any too soon. We arrived just before dark on a Tuesday, and his mother died that Friday. Green said he knew that she had just held off death until we got there. She had cancer, and I never knew anyone who died harder. The night before she died, the lady who was taking care of her asked me to take her daughter Cecelia out of hearing. I kept Cecelia out in the hills most of the night, and when we came back we were told it was all over. Howard was white and hardly looked like the same man. Green and Cecelia's mother were crying, and were not ashamed of their tears.

We built a box and took his mother to Boise. Howard was willed half interest in Dick Green's little ranch and eventually he and Cecelia were married.

I stayed around and helped with what I could for several days. One day we got to drinking a bit, and decided to run in some range cattle to ride, just for practice. I broke a lace on one of my stirrup leathers, but I was in a hurry to get back to riding, so I just made a quick repair for the time being.

I was short on cash, so I decided to go down toward Twin Falls to look for a haying job. I started out one evening on a little jug-bellied mare called "Skyrocket." (So named because she would go straight up at any excuse, and if you weren't watching she would fly at you just to get it out of her system.) About 2 A.M. I was in the high hills above Mountain Home. The moon was out, and the stars were chasing each other all over the sky. I was half asleep in the saddle when I heard a train whistle way out in the desert. It sounded miles and miles away — and I reckon it was. Its a sound never to be forgotten, and I would really like to hear one of those old-time whistles again, away out there. But it is only in memory, as the trains don't whistle like that nowadays; and no one nowadays is nuts enough to be alone in the middle of the night, miles from nowhere, riding old Skyrocket with one leg slung over her neck in front of the saddle horn, wondering if he had laced up his stirrup leather properly.

As I was thinking about it, I reached down and pulled up my right stirrup to make sure. But it was okay; I had fixed it properly. I just let it drop back in place and the old mare didn't like it; I picked myself up from the middle of the road. Skyrocket just backed up a little and snorted. I figured she just couldn't do that if I was expecting it, so I piled back on her, threw my leg over her neck, picked up the stirrup, and let it drop, and picked myself up out of the dusty road again. I still couldn't believe she could do it, and being dumb I crawled on her again, hooked my leg tight around the horn, grabbed the stirrup, slammed it down and crawled back out of the dust a third time! I was beginning to believe maybe she could do it after all, and I got back on. This time I put my knee over her neck, but kept my foot on the right side, figuring I could drop my foot back down and ride her. I took the stirrup and slammed it down, but she just kept on going down the road, I tried it several more times amd she didn't pay any attention to it. I picked up the stirrup one more time — I wanted to show her that she wasn't so smart — then I decided I was making a fool of myself. Without thinking, I slipped my foot back over her neck, dropped the stirrup, and she unloaded me again.

I have heard that it is not the bleating of a thousand sheep, each making a different sound, that makes a sheepherder go nuts — its turning their rotten square quilts around and around trying to figure out which way is the long way. I have wondered since what made me act that way, alone out there miles from no-place. Maybe I am improving, as I never tried it again. I have told about it a few times, and here I am writing about it; maybe I'm improving after all.

I did not find a job. It started to rain and there would be no haying jobs for at least a week, so I went back to Rattlesnake Creek, rounded up a bunch of broomtails and moved to lower country, looking for winter range. Down the Boise Valley in the town of Eagle I came to a livery stable and corrals. A fellow asked me if I had any trading stock, and I told him they were all for trade. I was riding Skyrocket, and I tied her up and went over to look at his stock in the corral. He had only one he would trade — a tall gray, quite a fine looking animal, but his hooves were long and turned up in front. The man wanted to trade for Skyrocket. I knew there

must be plenty wrong with the gray, but I couldn't see anything physically wrong, so we traded.

I was going to try the gray out, but the man said, "He is
yours, and the bill of sale is good, but you aren't riding him
here."

Just then a big fellow with a star pinned on his vest said,
"What's more, stranger, you are not going to ride him in this
town."

So I took my riata and roped the gray. He fought the rope
some, but not bad, then he whirled and came toward me,
nodding his head. I expected him to lay back his ears and
come at me, but he kept his ears forward and stepped high
in front, and I knew that he would strike. I ran the rope
around a corral pole and tied it, and went out and got my
pack and bell mare. (A bell mare is usually only packed with
your grub and bedding, and the rest of the pack animals are
tied to her. She has to be gentle, but tough enough to lick all
the rest of your stock. A good bell mare is a valuable animal.) I got my bell mare (Granny) up beside the gray, and
worked over her neck so he couldn't strike at me. I got a
halter on him and tied the halter rope to Granny, then
slipped the riata off his neck. He didn't seem to act very
tough to me, but I knew he must have been spoiled in some
way, as he should have been worth several of Skyrocket. I
led them around the corral a few times, then went out and
got a saddle horse, tied the bell mare's rope up, and they
went out with him leading like a dog.

I left the valley and got to Horseshoe Bend that afternoon, camping at an old mill pond. I tied Granny up, pulled
the new horse up close to her and put a pair of bronc hob-
bles on him and left him tied for the night. I turned the rest
of the horses loose to graze, but I wanted him to get good
and hungry and out of familiar country before I took any
chances of losing him. I called him Eagle, after the town I
got him in.

He broke loose in the night, and he and another horse
swam across the pond. There was a little current in the
pond, but there was a fence above it, so I couldn't go
around. I would have to ride across the pond. I saddled up a
buckskin mare I thought a lot of. (Her name was Buck, and I

had caught her as a wild horse on Hampton Butte, Oregon. Nature never did wrap up any more or better horse in that much hide. I had gotten wind of her as a wild horse that couldn't be caught, so naturally I had to investigate, and when I first saw her I just had to stack my twine around her neck. If I'm not mistaken, Reub Long, co-author of "The Oregon Desert," was one of many she flagged her black tail at as she disappeared over a hill.) I crossed the mill pond at a spot I thought was not too deep, but at the far side Buck went under, and she turned out to be the only horse I ever saw that couldn't swim. She just let her hind feet sink, paddled with her front feet and came over backwards. I had to go to the bottom to keep from being struck by her front feet. I had my mohair chaps on, and of course boots and spurs, and I doubted if I was going to come up again. But somehow I surfaced, grabbed some thorn brush hanging over the water, and got to the bank.

It was about four feet up, steep and slippery, and as I started to crawl up I looked back at the mare. She had righted herself, but was slowly floating toward the spillway, when one of her ladigo bridle reins came floating by. I stepped out as far as I could and just caught the end of the rein. I hung on and she drifted in to the bank and got her feet in the mud and held on there. I got her tied to a heavy branch of the thorn brush, then crawled around through the mud to where I could get my riata around her neck. Then I untied her rein and pulled her down the pond to where she could climb out. I rode around the two loose horses, and they both jumped in the water and swam right back to the other side. The hobble didn't stop Eagle from swimming. I had to take Buck upstream to where I could find a gate in the fence and a shallow spot to cross. When I got back to camp I roped Eagle and tied him up, and he acted pretty decent for a spoiled horse.

I built a big fire, got into some dry clothes, and hung my wet ones up to dry. I fixed myself some breakfast, and while I was eating a stranger came into my camp and had coffee with me. He kept looking at Eagle and asked me if I had had him long. I told him I had just traded for him the night before.

"Did they tell you anything about the horse?" He asked me. When I said no, he continued, "Then someone ought to string them up! As soon as you get him up in the hills you'd better shoot him. That horse has killed two men and injured another. He bucked them off and turned and jumped on them."

I told him, "It was probably their fault. The horse is too young to be a killer. He can't be more than three years old."

The man confirmed that Eagle was a long three year old.

I hit the road the next day, with Eagle tied to Granny's rigging. When I stopped for the day I started working with him. I snubbed him up close, roped his front feet and pulled him down on his knees until he quit fighting. Then I put the pack rigging on him and loaded him with my bed and some other gear. After a few days I could pack him without roping his feet, and by the time I got to Salmon Meadows he was my pack horse.

I landed a haying job with the E O cow outfit and turned my stock into a pasture there. It was a big ranch and we put up around eighty tons of hay a day. Osborn, the owner, was a retired jockey, and a real man. He had around forty head of registered Thoroughbred mares, and his stud was "Jocum" — the best imported blood at that time. As my life was mostly horses, we hit it off right away. He asked me where I was headed and I told him "bunch grass and winter range."

He said, "The Thunder Mountain country has the best grass I ever saw, but the Lower Salmon where you are headed is too steep, and lots of stock is lost by rolling off those steep hills. There is a fellow here by the name of Kid Garden, who is trailing fifty head of heifers in a couple of weeks. You could be a big help to him, and there is plenty of range in his country for your stock."

So he got us together. Garden said I could winter with him and his wife, and they would be glad to have me. Osborn said we only had to wait until the hay was put up. Everything worked out all the way around: Osborn got his hay stacked, I got some extra pay to winter on and range for my horses, and Osborn got his heifers trailed to the back country. The Kid, as everyone called him, was fifty-six at that time, but didn't look over thirty. He had been an outlaw in

When elk were plentiful in the back country of Idaho

Montana known as the "Yellowstone Kid," and he was proud of it. He got stuck on my Eagle horse and wanted to buy him. I told him the horse's reputation, and that made him want him even more. I really wanted to keep Eagle, so I put a high price of $75 on him, but the Kid pulled out the cash. I told him to just keep the money until I got Eagle broken or to buy grub with it, and I would help him eat it. Coin or paper money was just so much extra baggage back there then.

I don't remember how long it took us to trail into the back contury, but it was done without the loss of a single hoof, and the last couple of days the trail was really dangerous. Mrs. Garden was a really fine person, small and plump, and she thought a lot of everyone, especially the Kid. She was known as "Auntie" Garden. She was a preacher's daughter, and one of the happiest people I ever saw. She had two nephews living about a mile up the mountain from her — and I do mean *up*. Their names were Joe and Roy

Elliot. It was Joe's homestead, but Roy had half interest in it. Joe was "outside" working at a mine in Warren.

The "back country" of Idaho is that area now called the Primitive Area. It is generally the Salmon River drainage, northwest of Sun Valley, southwest of Bighorn crags, southeast of Warren and east of French Creek.

There were literally thousands of deer in that country; farther back there were elk, and bighorn sheep in the high country. In the extremely low country, the farther down you went fifty or sixty miles, the wilder it got. There were mountain goats, big horns, grizzly, black and brown bears; the streams were alive with trout, white fish, and salmon in season.

Everyone wore handguns, and there were people from all walks of life. There was a professional ball player (Jim Hackett), railroad men, miners, outlaws; one real gunman, Deadshot Reed, and "Uncle" Dave Lewis, who had been in the back country for fifty years when I came there, and was a true mountain man. There were two school marms and their families. There were far more people there then than there are today. It was a wonderful country then, but its like a lemon with all the juice squeezed out today. There was just too much "management" by "experts" who learned all they knew from books that were written by people who knew even less.

Roy was living alone and asked me to winter with him. We lived mostly on meat, spuds, and bannocks (trail bread) but at that we had plenty of everything. Roy was a good cook, and Auntie Garden would have us down now and then for a lot of extras. I ate my first cougar meat at her place, also mountain goat. Both are very good if cooked properly, but hard to take cooked over a camp fire.

That winter World War I began and the government called for volunteers, but it was impossible to get out at that time of year. They called for volunteers a second time in the spring. (The draft wasn't a law at the time.) I told Roy I was going out.

He said, "Go now, while the high snow is deep, before it starts breaking up. We can take a couple of horses as far as we can go on a warm day. Then we'll rest until about daylight when it freezes up and forms a crust to walk on. When we get to the top we can put the horses on guy ropes and let them down to softer snow and you can bog it out from there. Take a little grain and grub, and I believe you can make it. I'll help you over the top and down to the soft snow, and then it will be up to you. I'll have to get back over the hump before the snow starts to loosen up on top."

We got everything together, and smooth-shod the horses so they could travel when we got to the outside, and so they wouldn't cut themselves if they got to floundering in the snow. Next morning we pulled out for Edwardsburg. Mr. and Mrs. Edwards had a post office there in those days, but they are long gone how. About a mile below that now is the forest service headquarters, a landing field, hotel, grocery store and gas pump. Its only a little way from there to Big Creek, which is really a river. We camped about four miles from Edwardsburg, as that was the last grass that amounted to anything, and we let the horses eat. I was taking two mares out: "Buck," my Hampton Butte buckskin that couldn't swim, and "Bird," a bay Morgan-Thoroughbred cross. I was going to ride Buck and pack Bird. Buck was plenty smart, but Bird was dumb.

We were going to try to go over Logan Summit — something over 9,000 feet, not too steep on the north and east sides, but plenty steep on the west and south. We got into snow before we got to Edwardsburg, and we knew that it would deepen fast from there on. The sun was out, there was a light wind and the snow was pretty loose. We began to climb fairly fast, and the horses weren't having too much trouble. Roy and I took turns breaking trail, and we kept at it until about midnight. We tied the horses up and gave them a little grain. We took the pack off, but left the pack saddle on Bird and the saddle on Buck, to keep them as warm as possible. We stamped out a spot and started a fire, but it didn't do much good as the smoke was worse than the cold. Before daylight Roy and I tramped a trail out from the trees into the open. We wrapped gunny sacks around the horses' feet, three sacks to a foot, and led them out to the end of the trail. It was plenty cold, and a crust had formed on the snow. We could walk on it, but the horses broke through now and then. We should have had snowshoes for them, but the sacks worked as well, and the horses didn't skin thenselves up the way they would with snowhoes. It take quite awhile for horses to learn to use snowshoes, and I never saw one yet that didn't skin its legs all up from the knees down.

We took our time, climbing gradually. As we got higher, it got colder, and the crust was stronger. When we got to where the horses didn't break through anymore we moved as fast as possible. We wanted to get over the summit and as far down as we could before the snow started to loosen up. When we finally made the summit, we let the horses rest a bit. The other side of the mountain was too steep for a horse to go down by itself. We tied Bird up, led Buck out to where it got steep and tied two long ropes to her. With one rope we took a couple of wraps around a tree above her. We wrapped the other rope around a tree ahead of her, so if she fell we could hold her. Roy gave slack on the first rope while I led her downwards. As soon as she felt the support of the rope, she let it balance her and walked ahead as though she had done it all her life. We got her down to a spot where she could stand without slipping, tied her up and went back for Bird. We had tied Bird up at the edge of a snowslide trail. This trail was clear of timber all the way to the bottom of the steep side of the mountain, and from there on everything was covered up where the slide had gradually stopped. Those trails are hard packed and steep, to where they taper off at the bottom. We got Bird all rigged up, and I started to lead her down toward Buck. Roy eased off on his rope just a bit, but Bird did not trust us or the rope, and she tried to lean up the grade instead of using the rope to steady herself. Her feet slipped out from under her, and there was no such thing as getting her back on her feet. Roy tied his rope to keep her from sliding down, and that was that.

Roy scratched his head and said, "The foxes and marten will have a feast. But you will be cut of a pack horse, grub and bed."

I said, "I could get supplies on the South Fork, and I can get that far on Buck in a couple of days. I'm not going to turn back, but before we shoot her, let's try to slide her down. It can't do anymore than kill her."

Using our long ropes, we slid her out to the edge of the snowslide trail. We tied her feet together to keep her from struggling. Roy and I tied both the ropes securely so she couldn't go anywhere.

Roy asked, "What do we do now? Time's a-wasting, and its a quarter of a mile down."

I got a pack manty — a seven by eight foot canvas — and we worked that under her, tied it up over her side and back, I told Roy to cut the rope, and down the mountain she went! Roy had a half-grown shepherd dog that thought it was all a lot of fun. The pup started after Bird, his feet flew out from under him, and he went down without a manty. There was nothing to stop Bird until she got to the bottom of the slide, and she went out of sight where the slide had leveled off. We got my rigging and another manty, made a cargo of it and turned it loose. Then we worked Buck down the mountain with the ropes. At the bottom we found Bird, and she was all right. We cut her loose and she got up — pretty dizzy, but otherwise okay.

Roy said, "Good luck, Ed. I'll see you after the war." And he turned and started climbing back up the mountain.

I saddled up, riding Buck and leading Bird, I went from tree to tree. The going wasn't too tough — snow is always shallower under the trees. I made Elk Creek that night, and stayed overight with Warren Smith, and the horses had hay and grain. I had Warren Summit to make the next day, but it faced the sun and was bare ground almost to the top. From there on would be a road with packed snow, used by a mail carrier with snowshoes and shod horses.

I left Elk Creek and headed for Warren Summit, but I ran into a friend, Tom Carry, and he insisted that I spend a night with him. He didn't have to twist my arm too hard. The following morning I got an early start and got to Secesh Meadows and spent a night with Slim Fernard. He was also called "Stud," as the only horse he had was a grade work-horse stallion. He also had a pet mule deer he called Stinker. Fernard was a professional still operator, and he made really good moonshine.

I made Payette in five days, crossed the Snake River, and went to Dead Ox Flat where a real friend lived — John

Coats, a dairyman. I say a real friend, not that others weren't real friends, but because of what he told me just before he drove me to Boise to enlist:

"Ed, if you come back and are okay you will ride a lot of ranges yet — and that is as it should be. But if you should come back all shot up or disabled, come back here and make your home with me and my family."

CHAPTER 5

World War I

The army grabbed me up and put me into training under old Captain Boiss, the best drill master I ever saw. He saw something was wrong when I tried to do an about-face and almost swapped ends. Of course I was wearing high heeled boots, so he excused me until they could get me into shoes. I about had to learn to walk all over, and felt like I was going to cinch-bind and fall over backwards. The cords in my heels swelled up, so they laid me off and let me learn to wear shoes gradually.

We didn't do much for awhile, only I sneaked out and got to running the ridges and met a girl. She was a little thing, very good company, and before I knew it I had fallen hard. I thought she had, too, until she stood me up one night for another soldier. That did not go over too well with me, even though she tried to explain it all by letter. I figured she should have kept the date with me, and told me then if she had wanted to date someone else. Anyway, I didn't go out anymore, but stayed in camp licking my wounds. I figured if life in town was that way I would just have to take my medicine and make the best of it. I felt that a girl's word should be as good as man's. On the high desert, if your word was no good, neither were you. To tell the truth, I have not changed that way of thinking a hell of a lot, even today.

We were sent up to Northern Idaho to guard bridges. Our squad was stationed at Priest River and the folks up there received us with open arms and couldn't have treated us better. We had one knothead in our squad who was just plain no good and we all knew it. We told him that if he pulled one of his no good stunts he just wasn't going back, and he believed us. It was a good thing, because we meant it.

We got orders to stay in camp and be ready to move anytime, day or night. My sister Hazel and her family were living in Spokane at that time, and they sent me a telegram saying to come down; it was very important. Well, that put me up against a bluff with no trails around, and the fellows all took it about as hard as I did. Hazel and Joe had always stood by me, and I felt that I would be letting them down if I didn't go, but there I was, snubbed up by the Army.

Corporal Duncan said, "If it was any other time I would let you go and say nothing about it, but we are under orders to stay in quarters. I know we are going to go to Boise one day soon to join the rest of the 2nd Idaho Regiment before we go east. It's tough, but that's the army. . . ." He suddenly looked as if he had gotten an idea. "We will have to go through Spokane on our way to Boise. You go to Spokane now, but find out when this train goes through Spokane, and meet every train every day, without fail."

It was nearly train time at Priest River, so all the fellows got out their best clothes and uniforms and rigged me up proper. Duncan went to the train with me and saw me off. I landed in Spokane about 2 P.M. and hunted up my sister's house. She and Joe met me at the door saying, "Come on in, we have a surprise for you."

They took me into the living room, and there was the girl who had stood me up! She had told Hazel and Joe we had had a quarrel, but didn't tell them what it was about. There had been no quarrel, I just had never gone into town to see her again, and had figured it was all in the past.

Well, we were married the next day, two and one-half hours before train time. It turned out to be the troop train, and they picked me up, and no one ever knew about it. Corporal Duncan (Dunk) let the rest of the squad in on it, though. The black sheep of the outfit was not on board. I suppose he went over the hill; we never saw him again.

We landed in Boise and the rest of our regiment was mobilized and waiting for us to start east and into the war.

We went by train up into Canada, milled around and came back down through Philadelphia. We passed through the Italian section, where they had macaroni hanging on clotheslines, fences and wires, from string-sized to wide enough to make a draft horse harness. The train's smoke

Ed James during World War I

boiled through it, but it didn't seem to bother the people. They waved at the troop train and we waved back. They were dark-complected, and so was the macaroni!

We unloaded at Camp Mills, Long Island, and stayed there until we got to fighting each other, as soldiers will do when different companies are camped too close together. First maybe a couple of soldiers from different companies would get in a scrap, then it wasn't long before both companies were battling. They finally put on extra guard so we could get to town, and arranged it so the scrapping companies got leave at different times. Then we had to contend with the local gangs on the street corners. They were mostly Italians or Jews or a mixture of both — little scrubby looking birds who spoke every language but our own. They would take up the whole sidewalk, and people would have to step out into the street to go around them. But we did not go around them, and after a couple of trips to town they learned to move aside and give us room.

I had a little experience going to camp one evening. The train was crowded, as usual. Some of us had seats, but most of the soldiers were standing in the aisles. There was a little bit of a woman standing by my seat, holding a big, fat kid in her arms and trying to hold onto the strap. I got up and asked her to take my seat. She stood for an instant and stared at me as if I were some kind of curiosity, and one of those little dark-complected shrimps slipped into my seat. I got him by the back of the neck and hauled him out of there, and hollered to the boys to pass him back. They did, clear off the train, and not gently either. The motorman stopped the train and came back to see what the rip was. I tried to explain, but I guess I was a foreigner to him. All the fellows crowded down the aisle. I took the baby and told the woman to sit down. She did that time, and I handed her the kid. The motorman said that he would report us.

One of the boys said, "Go ahead, but if you don't want to follow that rat on out you'd better get back at your job, and sudden, because I can run this thing and probably do a better job than you."

He gave us no more lip, and we were on our way. That

woman didn't say a word, but she kept looking at me as if she thought I was a freak.

We were there about three weeks when one night about eleven o'clock we pulled out. You never know where you are going in the army. We arrived at Hoboken, New Jersey, and they loaded us on a boat. It was the *Trinadoris*, an English banana boat with an English crew, and the smallest big boat I was ever on. Not all of our company could get on, those of us who did were crowded, and that boat stunk. I was lucky, as I was stationed in the crow's nest, where the air was fresh. One hour on and three off, but I rarely came down except to eat. There were seventeen ships in the convoy, but by daylight of the first day out we were alone. They fed us soup, horsemeat and macaroni, all cooked in the same kettles. The horsemeat was coarse and tough, and for awhile most of it went over the side, until the boys gaunted up for a few days and got hungry enough to eat it. The bread was wonderful though, and we had marmalade to put on it, and it was good too, at first. After twenty-one days out of sight of land that marmalade went begging, it got to where we could hardly stand to look at it.

The boys below started to get seasick, so those of us in the crow's nest stayed up there as much as possible. It was early winter and the Atlantic was rough at times. The sea washed the little ship with three to six foot waves — it would go down into a trough, break through the next swell, and the mast would sway from side to side. We could look right down into the water, first on one side, then the other, and each time it felt like it would never come up again. Of course we were on submarine watch, but in the whole twenty-one days we only saw one freighter. I reported down the tube "man overboard" a couple of times, they answered, "man overboard," blew the whistle three short blasts and kept on going. There was no such thing as picking a man up in that sea, even if they could find him. The climate went from warm to cold and back again as we steamed all over the Atlantic dodging U-boats.

One morning I spotted something on the horizon, reported it, got an "okay" and was told to watch all around. I did, and there were spots in the sea all around us.

Whoever was taking my reports called back, "Good job, soldier! That is the British convoy of sub-chasers, we will be with the 'moiselles in a couple of days." (He meant mademoiselles.)

No doubt some of the convoy that had started out from Hoboken landed in England, but all of our regiment landed in Saint Nazaire, France. We all had sea legs by that time, and it felt as if the ground ought to roll and dip. I was on guard there for three days, while the ships were being unloaded. I couldn't understand a word of French, and the 'moiselles only knew one word in English. But like an old song said, you don't need to know the language unless you want to say goodbye. The French guards rudely kept the girls moving whenever they came around, and they didn't understand when we cussed them. "I don't understand," *pas compres*, was one of the first things we learned in French.

We left St. Nazaire and were taken back to our outfit. (I don't know where.) There the 2nd Idaho Infantry was to be a depot outfit. A depot brigade is a training unit, a skeleton outfit which takes on recruits, trains them, moves them on and takes in new recruits.

Captain Boiss had severe arthritis, and they would not let him go to the front. He was a tough old soldier, and the army was his life. He gave us a pep talk saying, "I will hold back any recruits who seem less likely to be able to take care of themselves. Men, I wish to God the higher-ups would let me go with you."

He started to call off our names, and tears started to blind him and his voice started to break. He had to turn the list over to 1st Lieutenant Regin, who went with us. I knew Regin clear into hand-to-hand fighting. In civilian life he was a preacher, and in military life he did not gripe and cuss like the rest of us. He was a real soldier and a real man. I don't know if he made it out of the war or not. Probably not.

We were sent up to the 2nd U.S. Army Pioneer Engineer's Regular Army. Some of us were assigned to Company E, and the rest were scattered out into the regiment. But no one would accept us, as mumps had broken out amongst us. We were billeted in tar-paper shacks, on wet ground with a little snow on top of the mud. We were given no special issue of food, and what we did get was very little. I spent my twenty-second birthday there. Of course it was Christmas, so they put out an extra effort for us. We had three turkeys. For 142 men. I know, because I was on KP that day and I had to cut them up. I would cut them up, then go back and cut up the cut-up pieces until I couldn't cut any more. The cook said to hell with it, and none of us in the cook shack had, or wanted, any of that mess. We ate hard tack and corned wooley, and we hated the sight of that.

We had three army blankets and a straw tick for a bed, but they forgot to give us any straw. The only positive thing about our surroundings was that they were just what the mumps needed to flourish, which they did. They finally began to send the very sickest of us to the hospital.

The reason we were treated so badly was that the men in the regiment were regular army, and we were 2nd Idaho, which had been a National Guard outfit before the war. It was about like bedding down a horse buckaroo in the middle of a corral full of sheep. I had tough luck, as it took me a long time to get the mumps, and in the meantime we had a drill sergeant herding us up, over and down a ridge. One day a captain came to look us over, and he didn't like what he saw. Costello was his name, and I still cuss him in my sleep sometimes. Anyway, he took over and had us training in heavy equipment with fixed bayonets. We had to go over the ridge, swap ends, come back down and stick some dummies. The Captain had a bright idea and made us "bear-walk" up the ridge on one hand and two feet, trying to keep our rifles out of the mud and snow, then run down and stick the dummies. He kept eating on us, telling us what a rotten outfit we were, and that the army should be, and was, ashamed of us, and he didn't use very good language. He told us that we should run down that hill showing a lot of pep and yelling. We tried it again and he ate on us some more, saying we didn't yell. Someone in the back asked what we should yell.

Costello said, "Yell anything, but yell like you mean it!"

We went back up, and by this time we were pretty wet and tired and cold, and most of us had gotten our rifles muddy. When we got to the top some big ape in the back did yell, and you could have heard him a half a mile away. He yelled, "I wanna go home!"

We had to go back to camp, clean our rifles for inspection, then hike in heavy marching order until eleven o'clock that night. Some had to be picked up by the ambulance, they were lucky the rest of us finally got back. Two days later I came down with the mumps and was glad of it. I was sent to Base 18, wherever that was, and put in a ward with about fifty other men who were down with the mumps. They were in all stages, from getting well to going to the boneyard. They fed us pretty well, and the nurses were American,which helped a lot. The only medicine I ever got was cognac, and that helped a lot, too. The nurse who brought in our food always made it handy for some of us to grab a few quarts of cognac, and she said that we were the thievingest bunch she had ever seen, but she smiled when she said it.

I was kicked out and put to light duty shoveling snow. The Frog who hauled the snow off had a cart with a team of three, in tandem, which was how they worked stock in France. He had one big jack, one camel, and one big Percheron mare.

It was only a couple of days before I was down again, and the mumps were down, too. I went through hell for a few days, and I was unconscious part of the time. The sawbones said he would have to operate to save my life, but I told him to go to hell. That riled him and he got to preaching his rank, and that really made me tell him off. Then he said he would operate anyway, and I told him that if he did he would have to dope me, and I would get him, when I came out of it. He left, and a nurse told me that I was very disrespectful, but they could not operate without my written consent. That made me feel better, although she told me that I would likely die.

I didn't, of course, and when I finally got well I went to the office to get discharged from the hospital. There were five of us waiting in the office, all strangers to each other, but all from the 2nd U.S. Engineers. When we were all discharged, there was no noncommissioned officer amongst us, so they happened to give me the traveling papers, put me in charge, told us how to get back to our outfit, and gave us some Frog money. An MP took us to the train and watched the Frog conductor lock us in. The conductor blew his whistle, the engineer blew his whistle, the conductor blew his whistle back and we went bumping down the line about fifteen miles per hour.

I put it up to the fellows that we get lost and see some of the country. I got no argument, so at the next stop we got out when the conductor unlocked the door, and boarded a train that was standing on another track. There was a Frog woman who rattled out a lot of Francais and we understood none of it. Then another conductor came along and jabbered a lot to us, and we just shook our heads. He went and got the first conductor and they waved their hands and told each other all about it, and tried to explain to us, and finally threw up their hands, shrugged their shoulders and parted. The new conductor tried again, but still we couldn't comprez. Finally he said something like: "American soldat beau cou, coo coo," and gave up.

We got down into Italy and a MP picked us up, looked over our papers, told us we were way off our trails and put us on the right train. He told us where to transfer and a lot of other guff that we made a point of forgetting, and we were on our way again. We passed a little villa, then stopped at a bigger place, but the conductor didn't open our door. We looked at our papers and decided our ride would soon be over if we didn't do something. I suggested we pile off and find another train.

"Lead the way," they said.

I found a window that I could get through, but it was small and we would have to dive out. We did; the others were lucky and landed on a grassy slope. I landed on a cinder shoulder and cut the heel of my right hand (I still have the scar), but what the hell, we were on our way.

We ran and hid in an unlocked car that we figured was going somewhere, and that was just where we wanted to go. It soon pulled out, and we crossed into Spain, got off at the first station that amounted to anything and ran plumb into an MP who was looking for us.

"Boys," he said, "all the MP's are alerted, with orders to escort you to your outfit. If I could, I would forget you and send you on your way, but they know which way you are headed, and I could get in trouble if I don't take you back."

We were escorted back to our outfit the next day, and I delivered the papers to an acting adjutant. He looked the papers over and seemed startled.

He grinned. "It was too bad you birds didn't get lost in some part of Alaska or the U.S. Do you know that you had your service records as well as your traveling instructions?"

I nodded. "I knew it — wasn't I supposed to?"

He said, "Hell no! No man is allowed to have his service record. If he should get away with it, he could turn it in years later and demand pay for as long as he had it. We can't arrest you because you didn't go A.W.O.L., but you knew what you were doing, and so do I. I would kind of like to have been with you."

At Souville we had a really good "Y" man (YMCA) which was surprising, as we didn't think there was such an animal.

One night he told us, "I'm going back to the States. They won't let me do what I know is right here, and I volunteered to come entertain the troops, not take advantage of them."

We got a new "Y" man in, and he proved to be like all the rest of them. The Knights of Columbus were always okay. The Salvation Army just couldn't have done more for us, and the Red Cross did a lot of good at that time. But the "Y" was not a popular outfit to say the least.

We were trained to handle explosives, then moved on to Camp Romaine, a short way from Brussels, into the first and only trenches that I was in. We worked timbering up dugouts, and repairing "duck boards," walkways in the bottom of the trenches, which were supposed to keep you up out of the water, but never made much difference, as we were mud images anyway. We slept in shallow water, and as long as the rats didn't bite you or jump in your face, all was okay. When they did, you grabbed a hobnail shoe (someone else's), threw it where you thought the rat had gone, and usually hit someone (not the rat), and the fight was on.

"Cooties," or just plain-old gray back lice, marched in columns when they weren't in your bed or your clothes. I remember at Camp Romaine we were sitting in as dry a spot as we could find, eating and trying to keep the rats out of our mess kits. A lieutenant came down through the men and a new recruit got up and saluted. The Looie asked him, not too pleasantly, what he wanted.

The recruit said, "I believe I have creepers, sir."

"What the hell are 'creepers'?"

"The men call them cooties."

The Looie said, "Oh, you think you are lousy?"

"Yes, sir. What shall I do about it?"

The Looie pushed past him, then looked back and said to the poor guy, "Scratch them, just like I do."

We were shelled every time we left Camp Romaine to go to the trenches no matter how often we changed routes, so we knew we had a Kraut sympathizer amongst us. One night I went out to examine my gas mask. (They got filthy and wet, and we hated them.) I saw a soldier looking over the other masks. He quit as soon as he saw me, and I went into the billet and reported it to the man in charge. He rushed out and found that the breathing tube in his mask had been cut in half. He yelled, and a bunch of fellows ran out and found their masks cut up, too. That bird just did not live long.

One day someone came in and said, "The "Y" must have had a change of heart. A couple of them are out there setting up a camp to furnish hot chocolate!"

We had not had a payday for over a month, and we were just starved for anything good to eat, especially sweets. When we got out to the "Y" stand, we found out they wanted a franc, about 25 cents, for two-thirds of a cup full of cocoa. Of course we all went back to our bunks bitching.

One of the fellows ran in and said, "Those S.O.B.s are pouring that cocoa on the ground!"

We went out in a bunch and surrounded the camp, but the birds had made their getaway. Someone had tipped them off, otherwise there would have been two less "Y" men. We mixed what was left of the cocoa and sugar together, and most of us got a dig at it. We threw the rest of the "Y's" stuff together and burned it.

We advanced the next day to a little village where the

Krauts had already been, and the sights there were too horrible to pass on to you. We were told it was done to intimidate the French, but nothing could have put us more on the prod. We were already sore at the "Y," the government, and some of our own officers. We got to where we believed no one but our immediate fellow soldiers. We were given a lot of bull, promises of food, clothing, relief and furlows, but nothing came of it, only more rumors. You either kept your mouth shut or someone shut it for you. I can see now that it was good training, and you were more likely to come back if the urge to fight was all that was left in you. In a battle you knew if you stopped you'd get it from behind, or from either side, so the only way to go was to clear a path in front of you and keep moving until someone ordered you to stop. You were trained until there was nothing left in your mind but to fight and to obey orders, and you did so without thinking.

We were being recruited constantly, but still our ranks just faded. Then came a point when there was no one ahead of us, and we were ordered to advance to just over the next little rise and dig in. We were in view of the Krauts and it was suicide but we did it anyway. The Marines came up behind us to the brow of the ridge and set up machine guns and some light artillery. The heavy artillery was farther back and was horse drawn. Those horses would come in on a dead run, whirl around and release the artillery without stopping, and the gunners started shooting through the horses' dust. We were being shelled from back of the Kraut lines and the ground was actually boiling with explosives.

Then I got mine. Shells came over and hit with little or no sound in all the noise of battle. Some of the French on one side began yelling "gassa, gassa" and running back. We had long since thrown packs, gas masks and most of the ammunition away. We had to be in hand-to-hand combat when we could only use trench knives and bayonets. The Marines held the line while we fell back, but we were all gassed, and many were shot up or shrapnel-wounded. We got behind the Marines to where the ambulances were coming and going, but there were too many badly wounded patients, so those of us who could still walk went back to the lines. In the heat of battle you lose track of everything except the blind urge to fight to the end, and adrenalin carries you through unbelievable situations. I was alone when I got back to the lines and I was stopped by a Marine Lieutenant who asked me where I was going.

"Company E, 2nd Engineers," I replied.

"There ain't any such thing," he said. "They're all shot to hell. Go down in that brush and snipe the spiked helmets (German officers)."

I started shooting from about 150 yards at officers, with the woods so full of Krauts that there wasn't room for all of them. When the Marines put over a barrage I would snipe, then lie still when they stopped. I was still there the last I knew.

I came to in a half-standing cement church, in a hall with a lot of dead soldiers. A doctor came along and asked me why I was there, and I asked him how in hell I should know.

He looked at me and said, "You are the gassed patient who was having such a hard time breathing, and your heart was about worked to death. I had them bring you out here to bump off. We were overworked, and I thought you didn't have a chance, but we all make mistakes. I'll have a pill roller come take you back. You might make it now, if you don't go blind. Your eyes are injured by mustard."

I could only see through a red blur, and I really didn't give a damn if I did bump off; my lungs felt like they were on fire.

I came out of it now and then, and I don't remember much until I woke up in an open air hospital in Paris. I gradually was able to see a little and the pain lessened a bit. I began to walk around and sit out on the wide parkway on Rue de Grand and learn a little French. I sure had a lot of sympathetic teachers, the 'moiselles made me feel like a big shot for once in my life.

After a few weeks I was sent to Blois, a big convalescent hospital. While there, I was asked if I would like to go to Someur, and although I didn't know where that was, I was glad to go anywhere. I was told that Someur was an artillery school, and they were having trouble with the American horses there. Some big shot veterinarian was inspecting and found that the French mounts were fat, but the American stock looked rough. They were looking over my records and had found that I was a stockman in civilian life. So I was sent there, along with a vet, to find out what was wrong. When we got there, the vet went to look at the horses, while I got acquainted with the French sergeant. It happened that he could speak a little English. He was a little fellow, and a typical Frog, but he had red hair, and I figured maybe there was an Irishman somewhere in his dim past. He was very friendly and helpful, and told me when the forage came in, hay went on both sides of the "chardonnay" (parade grounds) but the grain was all taken in the French side, so no wonder their horses were in better shape. The vet couldn't find much else wrong with the horses except that their feet were in terrible shape.

The next day a Captain Snow showed up, and the vet and I gave him our reports.

Snow said, "We have a lot of B-Class men back from the lines. We will get them down here and make an American outfit out of this."

So it was done; Snow sent to Blois, got a bunch of non-com officers, and formed a company. I did some riding instruction, and just sort of knocked around. I rode a lot of horses, but I didn't care much for the McClellen saddles, and the artillery saddles were worse. The Americans had confiscated fifteen head of Arab horses, (back on the high desert we would have called that just plain horse stealing) and they were for sale. The students officers bought them up at once, and I got the job of breaking them.

First the vet and I gelded them. They were mostly sorrels, and the prettiest shades I ever saw. Some of them were almost orange. I asked the vet if he could find me a Western saddle to break them with, and he said he just bet he could, that in the chateau there was a whole room full of tack, from elephant saddles on down. He got me a complete western outfit, and I went to work breaking those fine horses. I am not an Arab man, but those horses would have been top animals in any country. They weren't rattle-headed and obstinate like most of the Arabs in this country.

The French thought I was "coo-coo" to try to break a

horse alone. It took at least four and usually five Frogs to break a horse. They would take a horse into a big cement riding hall that had about twelve to sixteen inches of sawdust in it, put a halter and heavy longe rope on the horse, and a sort of back band with big rubber knobs on top, rather like a draft horse hames. They would hold the horse until the rider got on and got hold of the knobs. Then they'd turn its head loose and three or four Frogs would hang onto the rope and keep the horse going in a circle until he was played out. Then they'd let him blow for about half a minute and make him go in a circle in the other direction.

Some of the Arabs bucked a little, but they were an easy bunch to break. I found a black horse in one of the stables that the Frogs were packing water to. Every time they passed him they would holler, "Iyeee, Gallieo" and he would jump ahead, snort, and kick the kicking boards. (Heavy iron-bound boards three inches thick and eighteen inches wide that swung between each horse.) Gallieo's feet were grown out at least five or six inches longer than they should have been. I asked what was wrong, and a Frog told me he was "beaucou fauche, beaucou boxay" which meant he was mean and would fight. He was a Canadian horse, and had been sold to the Americans when they bought half the French stock. Most of the horses were more or less crippled from standing on the cement, but the black seemed to be sound, other than needing his feet trimmed. Captain Snow said for me to pick out a private mount, and to keep it private, so I picked Gallieo, and started to work with him. First I put him where the French stablemen were not around, and I told the Americans to leave him strickly alone, not to even stand and look at him. It took me several days, a half to three-quarters of a hour a day, to get up to him without getting kicked at. The third day I could walk into the stall next to him on the other side of the kickboards, and I stood there talking low to him, and put my hand on his neck just ahead of his withers, then up almost to his ears, and back to his hips. He watched every move I made, but he didn't kick or strike or lay back his ears. Instead he trembled and seemed to be afraid rather than mean. The fourth day I took the kicking board out so I would have more room and could gradually get up to him. The fifth day I untied him and turned him around in the double stall. He was afraid, but not mean, and I was in no hurry. In a few more days I could lead him out of the stables to drink. Then I put a saddle on him, working over the kicking board. He stiffened up and blew, but he didn't try to fight. I put a bridle on him and led him into a riding hall that wasn't in use. I led him around a little, then took hold of the horn and shook it. He never tried to buck or fight, and though he was still scared, he quieted down. Whoever had originally broken him had done a good job, but then he had been made a fool of by some Frenchman who was scared of him. I trimmed his feet and shod him and I had what I considered the best horse out of over 800 head in the school. In a month he would follow me like a dog. One day I came into the stable and he was gone! I went outside, and there was Lieutenant Harmott, a French riding instructor, watching his orderly (dog robber) put his saddle on Gallieo, who was nervous but standing.

"What do you think you are doing?" I asked the lieutenant.

"I am going to use him for my private mount," the Frog informed me.

I said, "Like hell you are!" I walked over, shoved the orderly back, unbuckled the hotcake saddle and threw it on the ground. Then I pulled the bridle off and threw it after the saddle. Lieutenant Harmott went right up in the air, and began to whip his leg with his bat and spit through his teeth and finally walked up to me and pointed his finger in my face and said, "I weeel have you punished!"

I was lucky because Captain Snow had stood there and watched the whole thing. Harmott spotted him, ran up to him and started to jabber at him in French.

Snow stopped him, saying, "Lay off! That horse is American property. The French spoiled him and couldn't do anything with him. Besides, you are not allowed to ride any American horse without permission. Hereafter you and any other Frenchmen are to stay away from that horse."

Captain Snow was the American adjutant of the base, and his word was law. After that Harmott never looked at me again, although we passed two or three times a day, and that was okay with me.

I gradually worked up to stable sergeant, which was the job I really wanted. I was practically my own boss and had a duty sergeant under me to see that the work got done. I had a room that I shared with five others over the stable. (We weren't supposed to be there, but in the army its not what you do, but what you get away with.) All I had to do was teach some shave-tails (student officers) how to ride one hour a day. I had a permanent pass and all the best wine, cognac and beer that I wanted; but all I wanted was to go home.

One afternoon 1st Sergeant Maloney (we were good friends) sent a runner down after me with orders for me to come to the office on official business. I went up, and he told me that he was going on furlow for a week and that I had been appointed acting 1st sergeant in his absence, and he had a grin on his homely map. He soon quit grinning, though. That evening he got a telegram from home saying his mother was very sick and they were hard up for money. So Maloney raked together his money and wired every cent home to Portland, Oregon. Then he went to headquarters and explained the situation. (What good was furlow when he had no money left?) They told him that there were six others to go on furlow with him, and he was in charge, being the ranking non-com officer; it was too late to change orders. (Which was a lot of bunk.) They said the government was furnishing transportation and expenses and he would have to go with them.

Maloney came back to our room very unhappy with the army and particularly Sergeant Mager at headquarters. (Captain Snow wasn't at the post just then.) Next morning he rolled out of his bunk and hollered to me that he had it all figured out. There was a duty sergeant on that furlow, and Maloney would see them onto the train, turn the papers over to the sergeant and put him in charge. We felt pretty good about his idea, so we had an eyeopener on it; then he pulled out.

When he got back he said everything was lovely. I asked him what I was supposed to do — to go back to my job?

He said, "That should be easy, all you do is ride a good horse and kid the 'moiselles."

But I was still acting 1st sergeant and I would have to be relieved of that before I could go back to that tough job of mine, and I asked him what the procedure was.

"Just send a runner over to headquarters with a report that 1st Sergeant Maloney has reported back for duty," he told me.

I did, and the runner came back with orders for me to put Maloney under arrest in quarters. Neither of us felt too good about that.

Maloney said, "It looks like I've messed up the nest for both of us."

They tried him in a summary court marshall for disobeying orders and busted him to a private. A couple of days later Captain Snow came back and told the company clerk to post a notice on the bulletin board that the stable sergeant had been promoted to 1st sergeant of Company A. So I lost my job that I wanted the most. They promoted Duty Sergeant Napolean Frix to stable sergeant. We all had a shot of cognac, but it wasn't because we were happy. Maloney still bunked with me and I did not put him on any duty. I saw to it that the next bunch that was due to go home had his name on the list.

We got a change of company commissioned officer, a Lieutenant Humel, who was a professional soldier, a regular army man and our acting captain. He didn't bother to look through my service record, except to see that I had volunteered in the 2nd Idaho Infantry, and they were State Militia, and the regulars thought about as much of them as a horse buckaroo thinks of a sheepherder's dog. When the call had come out there had been no draft, and I had been told to join in our closest military organization, and of course mine was Boise. Acting Captain Humel did everything to make it tough for me, not only in the office, but with the men too. A 1st sergeant's job is tough anyway. If I had put every man in the brig that I should have, I wouldn't have had any men left on duty. And if I had done everything a rotten officer like Humel told me to do, I'd have shot myself. I had to learn to lie and get away with it, and I often had to look the other way. I finally got this acting captain over a barrel: He put me on duty that he himself was supposed to do, and of course I had to obey orders. I could have taken it to headquarters, but no one hates a stool pidgeon worse than I, so I let it ride. Then one time I was protecting a soldier who had gotten in late from leave, and Humel was making it tough for me. I told him I knew nothing about this fellow getting in after hours; Humel wasn't sure, and I knew he wasn't, and I stood up for the soldier.

Humel said, "Sergeant, you know you are lying to keep this fellow out of trouble and you know that I know it, and you know that I can't prove it."

I just said, "Yes, sir."

He shook his head and said, "I'll get you sooner or later."

I asked him why he had it in for me.

"I'll tell you the truth," he snarled. "I hate any militiaman's guts and I'm proud of it. I'm a professional soldier and a regular army man and proud of that, too."

It would have been a pleasure for me to run a bayonet through him.

They sent in several lists for me to fill out for some of the men to go home. I recommended the fellows who were in the worst physical shape. They were all B-Class men and had been disabled one way or another.

I was inspecting horses — it wasn't my job anymore, but I liked to be around them and to get out of that office — when Captain Snow came along and said, "Its a damn shame we had to take you off this job, but we needed you where you are now. I want to know why you haven't put your name on a list of those recommended to go home?"

I replied, "There are others in worse shape than I am."

He said, "This outfit will soon bust up, and I want to see your name on the next list. You've got it coming — and that is an order."

I guess he didn't trust me, because the next list that came in already had my name written on it, and I got orders to report to the infirmary without equipment. I filled out the rest of the list, and went to gather up some of my personal things in my room. When I got back to the office acting Captain Humel was there, and I hardly got in the door before he lit into me:

"What's all this about you reporting to the infirmary? Have you picked up VD?"

I told him, "I don't lay out all night like I could prove some people do."

"I'd have you thrown in the guard house if you were still under my orders!" he yelled.

I got what little I wanted from the office and went over to the infirmary. I just couldn't realize I was on my way home!

A couple of hours later Humel came in and said, "Sarge, I want to apologize about the way I treated you from start to finish. I looked over your service record. You were a volunteer before there was even a draft, you saw active duty with the regular army, and I never even got to the front myself. I have been a heel and I would like to shake your hand."

I said, "I'm glad you found out that you are a heel. I don't want to shake hands with you, because under the same circumstances you will treat the next man the same as you did me. The sooner you get out of my sight the better I will like it." I turned and started talking to some of the other men.

I was examined by a bunch of doctors and they told me I was Class D and would be sent home in a hospital boat. We got going in a couple of days, and we were quite a mess. Some were on stretchers, some lacking an arm or a leg, some were in wheelchairs and others were trying to break crutches to ride. I was one of the lucky ones, I had both arms and legs and no bayonet wounds, even though I did spit up a little blood now and then.

We had been deloused at the infirmary, and we hardly got off the train at Brest before we were run down the chute again. They gave us a handful of slimy yellow paste they called soap and told us to keep it out of our eyes, which of course we couldn't and I'm telling you, that stuff made us fight our heads. The water was so hot that we had to run, and by the end of the chute it was ice cold, and they had the guts to tell us to hurry! They handed us a whole new set of clothing, even down to garrison shoes. We had forgotten that they made anything but hobnail boots. When we got all rigged up and looked almost human again, we found out that we were under heavy guard and couldn't even go out and run the ridges. They held us three days "for observation" then ran us through the delousing chute again, gave us another new set of clothes, and finally loaded us on a boat.

The boat was the *Leviathon*, which had been stolen from the Krauts, and she was the biggest boat on the open seas at that time. Her sister ship never got out of the German harbor, or they probably would have swiped that, too. The *Leviathon* was, if I remember correctly, 926 feet long and as wide as a wild bunch corral, with deck after deck. I was bedded down on the hospital deck, the second deck above the water line, and they really made me comfortable.

We got a pep talk from a Frog general — I believe it was Marshall Foch himself — I had seen him in Paris a couple of times; then a talk from General Pershing. I had heard him speak before at troop inspections, and usually Patton and the Prince of Wales were with him. The Prince was a funny little guy that anyone would have to like. General Pershing said we should not knock any outfit when we got home, that they had all helped as much as possible. He mentioned the Red Cross, the Knights of Columbus and the Salvation Army, and got a big cheer from all over the ship. Then he said the YMCA, and he got a boo from the entire ship, and the booing kept up until he walked away. We were confined to quarters for showing disrespect. At the end of three days we shoved off, or there might have been real trouble; but when that big ship pointed her nose west everyone looked ahead and nearly forgot the past, for the time being anyway.

I had embarked from the United States November 26, 1917, and returned February 11, 1919.

The trip home was nothing like the one going over had been. We had good grub, good beds, and nothing to do but lie around and fatten up. The ship hardly swayed, and we were all basking in that grand feeling that we were going home and "le guerre" was behind us.

The fourth day out, as we were going to mess, at a turn in the gangway there stood a "Y" man trying to hand out candy bars. There were cripples in the line, and progress was slow.

The man ahead of me looked at the "Y" man, and said, "You are a little late in passing out candy, if you think you are doing us a favor you're wrong, and you'd better get out of here or you and that GI can of bars are going over the side."

The fellow believed him, and he disappeared and that can of candy went overboard. I actually felt sorry for him, because I figured he didn't know what it was all about, but I wouldn't have lost any sleep if they had thrown him over.

When we said howdy to the Statue of Liberty I heard one fellow say: "I am plenty glad to meet you again, but if you ever see me again, you will have to turn around." I felt the same way.

CHAPTER 6

Welcome Home

When we docked at Hoboken I don't believe there were fifty people there to welcome us home. We had heard of banquets and celebrations and had expected something better. Instead we were held on board overnight, then turned loose down a chute with barbed wire sides and Marines guarding it with fixed bayonets. This didn't make us happy. Some nut yelled out to the Marines, "Who won the war?"

One of the guards answered back, "Who stayed home with your girls while you were gone?"

We would have taken him apart, bayonet and all, but we had no chance to get at him. They kept us in confinement that night and the next morning ran us through another delousing. We were held three more days for observation, then I and some others were sent to Camp Funston for more observation. They examined us once a week for how long I don't know; I don't like to think about it.

The last time they told me I would be held another two weeks, I told the doctor, "You'd better do something. I volunteered for the duration, and that's long past. If something isn't done I will follow a lot of the others over the hill. If I have to ride the rods, I'm still going home."

He told me he would talk with me the next day, and for once he kept his word. He told me that they had been "observing" me for my own good, but that if I would sign some papers to the effect that I was okay physically, he would see to it I was discharged. I told him to trot the papers out, and I signed them, which of course was just what they wanted.

The next day I was finally turned loose, and I was on my way west, home to Idaho. Even if I did still spit up blood once in awhile, I was plumb glad to be free. I had lost confidence in the doctors, the government, and everything else but Idaho and home.

I finally got to Jerome, where my wife was living with her sister and brother-in-law, and there I did get a welcome that kind of drained the hate and disappointment out of my system.

I stayed about six weeks and then hit for Payette to see my friend John Coats and his family, and no one was ever more sincerely welcomed back. Today, while they have probably all gone over the "Great Divide," I still thank them for taking a lot more hate out of me. I stayed a few days and then headed for the back country. I got to McCall and from there took the stage toward Warren. We had to leave the stage and horses at the Half Way House because the snow was too slippery for the horses to stand up on. Al Stonebreaker was the stage driver, and he asked me to help him pack the mail. We made Squaw Meadows, and Al wasn't feeling too well, so he laid over there, but I was raring to go on, so I shouldered my pack and some of the mail and got to Burgdorf before dark. Old Mother Burgdorf came out of the lodge, gave me a once-over, yelled for her husband, jumped off the steps, grabbed me up like I was a two year old and packed me in the house. I weighed around 185 pounds — I think she was the biggest, strongest woman I ever saw, and she must have been in her fifties then.

She said, "I'm so glad to see you that I can't do anything but sit here and watch you! To think that you are back, and all in one piece! I'm going to go and get a feed on like you've never had before."

She did just that, and I couldn't begin to eat it all. Old Paw Burgdorf was a little fellow who ate like a bird, and he just looked at me and grinned. Next day Al Stonebreaker came and delivered some of the mail, then went on to Secesh Meadows and told me to bring along the mail when I came. I finally got away in a couple of days and went to Slim Fernard's. There was a young fellow wintering with him called Smith, and I hardly got in the door when Slim told Smith to go get us a drink. Smith came back with a jug and Slim said, "Hell, man, you didn't go down to the old cache and back already! This is Ed James! Get the hell out of here and go dig up the good stuff."

Slim still had Stinker, the mule deer, only now he was a

big buck, with big knobs that would be a nice set of horns by the following summer. Slim kicked Stinker out of the kitchen and began to bang pots and pans.

"Hell, Slim, don't fix too much," I said. "Mother Burgdorf just about foundered me while I was there."

He roasted several "fool hens" (brown and white speckled grouse called Franklin's Spruce Grouse) he had frozen outside, made gravy and baked bannocks, got out some huckleberries from under the floor in his cellar and made a couple of pies. While I was in France I had wondered if I would ever see grub like that again. I stayed one day and left the following morning, and Slim was almost mad at me because I wouldn't stay the rest of the winter with him.

I got to Warren that afternoon and the first person I met was Warren Smith. He just stood and looked at me. Then he said, "Word came in from McCall that a stranger was headed this way, and I came from Elk Creek to head off whoever it was, as we are in business back there and just can't have strangers in here this time of year. You've just got to come to Elk Creek and stay with me and Jim Hackett."

We stayed at the hotel in Warren that night, and no one would take a cent from me, and they really made me welcome. We topped Warren Summit about ten o'clock the next morning, took a trail down the other side and came to the Billie Duston Ranch. He and his wife just wouldn't hear of my going on that day.

Warren said, "I have to get back to Elk Creek. Jim will be worrying and wondering if I've gotten in a scrap."

So he pulled out and I stayed with the Dustons that night. The next day I went toward Elk Creek, but ran into Tom Carry, waiting at the South Fork Bridge. We shook hands, and he said, "You've gotta stay awhile."

"I promised Warren that I would be there tonight." I told Tom.

"To hell with Warren and Jim. You just gotta stay with us a few days. What would Janie say if I let you get by here without at least staying overnight?"

So I stayed overnight and went on up to Elk Creek the next day. I stayed with Warren and Jim about a week. Warren was the first white kid born in that country, and incidentally, the best shot with a hand gun that I ever knew. It was unbelievable what that man could do with a gun, although he wasn't considered a gunman, like several others in there — Kid Garden and Dead Shot Reed, for instance. Jim Hackett had been a professional ball player, and he could knock a grouse's head off with a rock.

I hit the trail and got over Elk Summit without any trouble and stopped at Edwardsburg to say hello to Mrs. Edwards and her son Nape, then stayed overnight with John Rouston and his family. I made the Garden Ranch the next day and found out that the Kid had died of the flu while I was gone.

I went from there to Cabin Creek, where Arch Bacon and his family lived. Arch had made me a deal to take over his ranch and cattle when I got back from the war, as he and his family wanted to get out; they just weren't mountain people. I told him I was still interested, but I wanted to bring my wife in as soon as we could get horses over the hump of Elk Summit.

While at Someur, France, I got acquainted with a man named Gabe Homsley, and he was all for coming in with me on the Bacon Ranch deal. He had a girl he was going to marry and bring in. I had told him about the back country and the game there, and he was all for it until I told him about the fool hens that you could kill with a three foot stick. He said that he had never doubted me, but he just could not swallow the fool hen story. I told him I'd prove it to him when he came.

I knocked around until the snow on the summit got down enough for the horses to bog out, and I helped the Bacons out, which made a good trail over the summit. I wired my wife to meet me at McCall, went on to John Coats to pick up Buck and Bird and my rigging, and meet my wife as planned. She was a city girl and had never been on a horse and knew nothing about the back country, but I had high hopes, and she did not disappoint me. She was game and a good sport and was really excited about the whole deal. I want to say here and now, no man ever had a better pal than she proved to be in all our time in the back country. We took it easy so she didn't get too sore and tired from riding. We had a really wonderful trip back and she seemed pleased with everything.

When we got settled I sent for Gabe, and when I met him in Warren the first thing he said was, "Now show me those fool hens."

We camped that night on Warren Summit and we saw some big blue grouse and he said, "Now let me see you kill them with a stick!" And he almost fell over laughing.

We camped next at the other side of Elk Summit down in the spruce country. I spotted five fool hens sitting on a low limb and pointed them out to Gabe.

"How many can you eat?" I asked him.

He still thought I was handing him a line, so I told him that a couple apiece should be enough. I got a stick and knocked off the hen on the furthest end of the limb. Of course the rest looked down at the one on the ground and began to cackle, then I knocked the next one down, and the next, and the fourth one flew down to the ground and ran behind the tree. I just reached around and knocked it over. Gabe stood there with his mouth open, then came over to me and said, "Ed, you can tell me anything now and I'll believe it."

Gabe had ridden a little in North Dakota and thought he was pretty good, but said he needed a little practice and asked me if we had anything that could buck a little. I knew of one that would be good to start with, so the next day I caught it and shod it for him. I had just finished when Gabe came in. He looked at the horse and began to laugh and asked if that was the best I could catch. I told him he would change his tune when he saddled him up the next day and tried to ride him. I told Gabe to put the horse in the barn, but instead he led it out and jumped on bareback. On the second jump he landed in Cabin Creek, sitting in water up to his armpits, yelling like a mashed cat. That water still had floating ice in it.

"You'd better go in the house and put on dry clothes," I advised him. "Up here in the high country a cold can turn to pneumonia quick, and that means death here; people just don't get over it."

He didn't argue. He did finally get to where he could

ride that horse with a saddle, but he couldn't fan him — every time he swung his arm he'd get piled up. That horse taught him a lot about riding, but not enough. Gabe was killed in later years trying to ride mean horses. He never should have tried to ride, as he was what we called a "blind rider" — he rode on nerve and balance, but he didn't use his head and got easily rattled.

Everything went along well that summer, we put up more hay that year than had ever been put up on that ranch, and Gabe was a lot of good help. We got all set for winter, and it came early and hard, and lasted until it put all the stockmen in that country out of business. The Kid Garden Ranch lost every head of cattle, the Able Ranch lost seventy or eighty percent and we lost fifty percent. We managed to keep feeding a month longer than anyone else and we threw dirt on the hillsides to melt the snow and still we lost half our cattle. The horses climbed the western slopes of the mountains where the snow wasn't crusted and pawed through snow up to their shoulders to find food. They came out in poor shape in the spring, but they made it. Cattle will nose into snow up to their eyes and then quit and starve to death, or they'll try to climb mountains looking for food and roll off and kill themselves.

That summer Gabe went out and got his wife, but she was from North Dakota and just couldn't adjust to the mountain country; in fact she wouldn't even try, and that put Gabe in a tough spot. We had a long talk, and I advised Gabe to take her back to North Dakota, which he did.

It wasn't a good growing year that summer, and I had a tough job putting the hay up alone, as I had to cut it by hand and rake it up with a pitchfork.

That winter, on a cold, clear night, the stars were twinkling and the lodgepole pines, frozen to their hearts, were popping like gunshots. It was a good time to be by the fire, and we were hoping that this would be the last cold spell of the season when the phone rang a loud, continuous call which meant for all us natives to get on the line; someone needed help.

Jim Hornburger was on the phone telling that Old Matty Mayhan had blood poisoning in his leg and had to be taken

Part of Big Creek Canyon from the air, looking almost straight down

out [of the back country]. That meant manpower, as there were no work dogs in there then. I got my skis out and told the Mrs. that I would be back as soon as I could. It was around twenty miles to Matty's digging and poor skiing on a crooked, rocky trail. I got into Matty's before midnight and found Roy Elliot and Nale and Emit Rouston, sons of John, there ahead of me.

Old Matty was lying on a bunk with his foot propped up higher than his head, his leg all bandaged up and his foot wrapped up with a hot water bottle. I asked what the idea was and was told that they had gotten through to a doctor in McCall and he said to keep an ice pack on the leg and keep his foot hot. In that weather the ice pack was easy, but then we had to figure out how to keep his foot warm out on the trail.

Roy spoke up. "I will see to that. It will be a slow drag, and I will go ahead of the rest of you and heat salt blocks."

Salt will hold heat a long time when wrapped, and of

course Roy, like all of us, knew how to build a hot fire quick in the dead of winter. Look on the north side of fir trees and you will always find limbs and twigs that are dry even in wet weather. Of course, then it was freeze-dry weather, at least fifteen below zero.

Jim Hornburger was on his way to Matty's bringing his big team of work horses to pull Matty as far as horses could bog through the snow. Just before daylight "Bearpaw" Brown showed up. I never knew another name for him, he always wore bearpaw webs and the handle stayed with him. He had his two rat terrier dogs, Toots and Ki-Yi, with him under his Macinaw. He packed them every place he went. He had never been to Matty's diggings and had been afraid he'd pass it up in the dark, so he had kegged up in the snow within 300 yards of the cabin and didn't know it was there. It looked as if he had had a pretty rough night of it; his beard and moustache were all caked with frost and ice, but Toots and Ki-Yi were warm under his Macinaw next to his hide. Bearpaw said he had just shivered himself into a sweat and sorta laid dormant the rest of the night. That was one man who needed about three fingers in a washtub of whiskey, but no one but Old Matty would take a drink. We didn't know how tough a job we had ahead of us, but we did know the back country. Whiskey or coffee will let you down in that high, cold country, but hard boiled strong tea will stay with you. Its hard to take, but it does the job and keeps you going.

Jim Hornburger showed up with his team of horses shortly before daybreak. Jim was one of those fellows who knows his way around. He pulled off Matty's bandages to redress his leg before we started out. The leg was bruised with black and blue spots from the knee to the ankle.

Jim turned to me and asked, "Ed, what do you think of it?"

I said, "I have kept on a job of riding with a worse looking leg than that."

"I figured the same," said Jim. "Matty, it looks like you want an easy way out in the dead of winter, no matter how much work and trouble you cause someone else."

Old Matty started to bawl tears as big as colt tracks. Jim

shook his head and said, "Hell, I'd let him stay here and rot if it was up to me."

I said, "Hell Jim, if Old Matty should croak we would kick ourselves the rest of our lives."

Jim said, "It sure burns my guts but I guess you are right, Ed. Out he goes."

There were still tears running down Old Matty's face. Jim told him, "dry up or your face will freeze!"

We rolled him up in blankets, packed him out and laced him onto the toboggan. I tied my skis on the toboggan as I intended to come back as soon as the job was done. The toboggan was made of a fresh deer hide with skis laced under it and a tarp and several blankets on top. The deer hide is placed hair side down and you pull the hair so it will slip over snow, brush or rocks. Roy went ahead on skis to build fires and heat the salt blocks. Jim hooked the team onto the toboggan in tandem and led the lead horse and the rest of us went ahead on webs, breaking trail. We only got about two miles when the horses began to flounder and Jim had to take them back. It was up to us from there on. Roy wrapped a block of salt on Matty's foot and we tied a rope to the toboggan with two cross poles. Bearpaw and I got behind the back stick and Emit and Nale took the lead pole. Roy pushed as best he could to get us started. There was some new snow on top of a crust or we could not have gone anyplace. Even so, it was a man-killer. At least we did not get cold, working hard. It was around 7,000 feet and we had to go about six miles to Elk Summit, at 9,000 feet. We all wanted to knock Old Matty in the head before we got there, and I still think it would have been a good idea.

We made the summit a little before dark, and Bearpaw and I pulled in front while the others pulled on a rope behind the toboggan to act as brakes and hold it back. It was easy going down hill to what was called the smoke house, a mail carrier's shack. We unlaced Matty and packed him into the cabin and the boys started a fire. The shack soon lived up to its name — the fire was built in the middle of the dirt floor and there was only one small window and the door for the smoke to get out. I figured I could make it back home by daylight the next morning, and I was all ready to hit the trail when Brad Carry from the South Fork drove up with a team of mules and a buckboard. While they were loading Matty on, Brad asked me how bad he was. I told him what Jim and I thought about his condition.

Jim cussed a little under his breath. "It sure as hell won't be a soft ride on a toboggan from here on. These hardtails are rarin' to get out of this high country and the road is full of rock.

I got back before I had expected and found everything okay at home. I slept the most of a couple of days, and I knew that was one trip I would never forget.

I wish that was all of that trip there was; the rest is worse. One of the Rouston boys took a cold that night at the smoke house and hit the trail for home the next morning. I don't remember which of the boys it was, but their dad, John, met them up Big Creek with saddle horses and took them on back home. The boy's cold turned into pneumonia, and that is death in that high country. To drag him out of there with pneumonia in that weather was just not possible. Of course everyone on the phone line knew about it, but there was nothing we could do. George Stonebreaker, over in the Chamberlain Basin country, had an old "Jenny" — a World War I biplane, and he webbed it thirty miles over to the Rouston's to see if it was possible to land on Rouston's place. He looked it over and told them to clear some boulders out, that he could land and they would see about getting out afterwards. George webbed back to Chamberlain, flew over to Rouston's and landed. They turned the plane around by hand and backed it up with a saddle horse as far as possible.

George said, "There's a fifty-fifty chance to get out."

John argued, "There's no use killing two men trying to get one out."

George said, "To hell with that. The boy will die laying here, and if he is willing I am going to try to get him out."

They talked to the boy, and he felt as his dad did, even though he realized he would die there. So it was up to George. They loaded him on the plane, George warmed 'er up good and took off. There is a fifty foot drop-off at the end of the run. They went over that and down out of sight. They showed up again farther down the river, their wheels just above the water, and then went out of sight around a bend. Finally they came into view again, and the plane was airborne! They got the boy to the hospital and he recovered.

Matty came back in the next spring and hollered Jim out. They had been good friends before, but Jim figured Matty really did want an easy way out that winter, so he told Matty never to darken his door again, that that wasn't a healthy country for him. Matty took his advice and made tracks out of there. I never saw Matty again.

My wife was soon to bear our first child and I had no help, as the nearest woman neighbor was seven miles down Big Creek. Big Creek is really a river, and is mostly white water, and dangerous. There were seven crossings in the seven miles. I delivered the baby and we named her Althaea. Three days later May and Johnnie Conyers came up. They hadn't been able to get to us any sooner because Big Creek had been too high to cross. Johnnie had to go right back, but May stayed with us for three days and helped out with the baby. Those are the kind of people a person never forgets. Big Creek started to rise again, and May had to leave, so I saddled up and rode home with her to make sure she got across okay. We made it, although we had to swim the horses part way across, and there was floating ice in the river. I was wet and cold when I got home, but glad to get back to the wife and daughter. I worried terribly about them, because if anything happened to me they could expect no help, and the phone lines were down. But I was young and capable, and used to taking care of myself and those who depended on me.

The Bacon Ranch was a losing game, so we moved up to John Rouston's place to put up his hay. He and his family had moved outside, and John was packing the mail from Warren to the Kid Garden Ranch. I was acting postmaster, and John would bring the mail to the post office and dump it on a table, then people came in and sorted through it and took their own mail. I went in now and then to get my own mail, to make sure there were enough stamped envelopes, and to make out a report stating that John had completed another trip. He got paid $50 per round trip, which took two weeks.

I stayed and fed John's cattle that winter, and sometimes took his place packing mail. We used dogsleds to pull the mail, unless the snowslides were too treacherous, then we cached all but the first class mail and packed that on our backs. John used webs (snowshoes) and I used skis. I took some long, hard falls on skis, but I never injured myself seriously.

The following summer our second daughter, Ethel, was born. I delivered her, too, and it was several weeks before any woman but her mother saw her. My wife wasn't in the best of health, so we decided to get out of the back country and hunt a new life.

CHAPTER 7

Jerkline Teams, Donkey Logging
and
Arkansas Moonshine

We had two saddle horses and two workhorses, and we rode out to the Payette Lakes near McCall, traded for an old buckboard and something that resembled a patched up harness, and pulled out. We eventually arrived at Fall River Mills, California where Bill, Ivadell and Gordon lived.

The Pacific Gas and Electric Company was putting in tunnels from Fall River to Pit River, and building power plants on the Pit River. They had bought up all the individual private power plants, as well as the telephone lines, which were just insulators nailed to the top of fence posts, with barbed wire for phone lines. I got a job as trouble-shooter. Stock kept knocking down the fences and fouling the phone lines. I bought up chickens on my trips while repairing phone lines, and made a few dollars selling them in the construction camps. Late that fall a line crew put in regular telephone poles and wire and that ended my job.

Bill had sixty head of big draft horses for construction and freighting, and I got a job from him driving a jerk-line team, pulling what they called a truck and trailer. We used sixteen head of work horses, strung out two abreast. I rode the near wheel horse (left side, closest to the lead wagon.) I had a rope running up to the near lead horse, which was attached to the off (right) lead horse by a "jockey stick" (a five foot pole snapped to each of the lead horse bridles.) There was a "bull" chain from the axle of the "truck" (lead wagon) to a ring on a short chain on the end of the wagon tongue, and on up to the stretchers on the lead team. (Stretchers are like double trees only made of iron, and the singletrees are attached to them, then to the horses.) The wheel team is hitched to the wagon like any other work-horses, but the two swing (middle) teams have their stretchers hooked to a ring on the bull chain, and are controlled by the stretchers and a jockey stick between them. The swing teams can't go ahead too far because of the lead team in front of them, and they can't lag behind because the team in back will bite them. The lead team is always well-trained, and they will swing wide on turns or get jerked by the driver on the jerk line. The swing teams soon learn to jump the bull chain as it swings on turns, or it hits their legs hard. The whole team is kept moving by the driver using a horse whip or throwing rocks. It isn't long before the bull chain never touches a horse, and you seldom have to throw a rock. They learn to climb a bank on one turn, and lean out over a bluff on the reverse turn. The horses weighed from 1,600 to 1,800 pounds and could pull unbelievable loads. An experienced jerk-line team is something to see in action.

Work was irregular; I freighted off and on all winter, broke and gelded a few horses, and worked in a slaughterhouse occasionally. Then spring came and we hit the road for the mouth of the Russian River. There I got a job in the Redwoods. There were about a dozen of us looking for a job, and I was last in line. The superintendent, MacVay, turned them all down, and when he got to me he asked, "Are you a logger?"

"Hell, no," I answered. "I don't know a damn thing about logging, but I do know how to work."

He looked me over and said, "Its a relief to run into someone who doesn't know all about logging. We'll take you on and maybe we can teach you something. Its impossible to teach anything to these know-it-all bums."

It was all donkey powered logging. MacVay took me up to the yarding crew and introduced me to the bull, who was called "Hambone." Hambone took me to the end of the yarding line and told me to stand back and watch. He waved to the donkey puncher, who pulled the line up, and Hambone followed it to some logs, put the choker around one and signaled the puncher. The line tightened and the log came off the steep hill and on down into the canyon where the bull line was.

The bull line was hauled back up from the donkey engine and when it got to us Hambone hollered "Ho" and the whistle punk whistled one short blast, the donkey below answered and the line stopped. Hambone jumped down, took the yarding choker off and put the bull choker around the tree. Then he got back out of the way and hollered "Ho, ho." The bull donkey answered the whistle punk with two blasts, the line tightened up and we could hear the friction slip on the big donkey's spool. He signaled back with several short blasts, Hambone yelled "Ho" to the whistle punk, jumped down and got slack in his choker. He then came running back and said to me, "Get back, because this is dangerous."

He signaled the punk to go ahead ("ho, ho") and the line tightened up. That big three and one-half inch bull line came off the ground and stretched and quivered like a fence wire in a blizzard. Then the friction down on the big donkey slipped and the much-repeated signal came up to us: Get Clear!

Hambone just stood there and grinned. "Something is going to come loose. A donkey puncher hates to be stuck, and that old Willamette donkey is powerful, and Monty Rose is mad." (His name was Montrose, but everyone called him Monty Rose and he hated it.)

Then we could hear the donkey signal several short blasts, and the donkey was running fast.

Hambone told me, "Monty is getting slack to make a run at the bull line."

The line loosened up and fell to the ground. The donkey was down the canyon and around several turns — we couldn't see it, but we could hear it speeding up until the hills and canyons seemed to vibrate. The bull line jumped off the ground, the choker tightened around the tree, gave a jerk, and the butt end of the tree came loose from the rocks, and the tree began to slide down the canyon.

We followed it down a couple of hundred yards, and the tree slid faster than the line was going, the choker loosened up and the tree hit a bluff and stopped. Hambone hollered to the whistle punk and the pull donkey stopped. We ran and jumped down, got the choker off and slid it up as far as possible, passed the loose end around in front of the log, hooked onto the bull line then got out of the way and signaled the whistle punk to signal the donkey to go ahead.

Hambone said, "It belongs to the bull line crew from here on."

We went back to where we had started, and McVay was there. Hambone waved to the yarding donkey and followed the yarding line back up the hill.

Mac told me to stay with him, that Hambone would not be back. "Your job is to take the yarding choker off the tree that is pulled down, send the choker back up, put the bull line choker on the tree and send it down to the bull line crew below. We call that setting and chasing. We usually lose or cripple a man or two each year, but its mostly their fault. They either get careless or scared and do the wrong thing. Always make sure the right signals go through and are answered by the bull donkey."

It was fast, hard, dangerous work, but there was plenty of time between logs to get your wind. My job was to keep the logs moving, and I kept one eye out for myself and one for the company, unless something went wrong, then it was both eyes for myself and to hell with the company.

One day the tail came loose on the haul-back line and killed three men. We packed them out and laid them out of the way at the landing and went on working. At quitting time they were loaded on the logging train and hauled out with a train load of logs.

Spring came along and I heard from MacVay that a dude rancher had some dairy stock that had gone wild, and a wild three-year-old stallion which he wanted off the range. I went to see the rancher and got the job.

MacVay told me, "I'm sorry to see you go, you've done your job well. But you have been lucky, and I'm glad to see you out of it before you get killed or crippled."

I went to work on the Glen Alpine Ranch. The owner was a vice president of the American Trading Company in San Francisco, and he used his ranch as a hideout from his office. He was a strict vegetarian, an exceptionally smart man, and also a nut. He would come up to the ranch and run around the hills naked, then come in all scratched up, his feet bleeding, with a sheet wrapped around him.

The deer were eating up the garden, and the birds were

eating the berries, but he said we would just have to raise enough for them and us, too.

His wife got me off to one side. "You're running things here, and as soon as Mr. W. leaves, you do whatever you feel should be done. But don't hurt his feelings by having meat on the place while he's here."

I soon rounded up the cattle and had them butchered, and he wasn't any the wiser. I trapped the stallion in a corral that I baited with a mare, and gelded him, and my job there was finished.

My son Ed was born there, and I had to deliver him. The doctor showed up too late, and when he did come, he looked our son over and remarked that I could have cut the cord a little shorter, but otherwise he looked okay. He never even took his diaper off. He had the nerve to tell me that he had come late because he had had an "emergency," and that I could pay him there and then and save myself a trip to his office. Well, I paid him and never saw him again.

My oldest brother, Steve, lived in DeQueen, Arkansas, and was in the plumbing business. He had shops in De-Queen, and in Idabell and Brokenbow, Oklahoma. He wanted me to come and take over one of the shops and learn the business. So we went to Arkansas, and while I didn't become an expert plumber, I sure had a time down there. It was during prohibition, and repairing stills was a big part of the business as far as money was concerned.

Steve and I were going over a rise one day in his Dodge, when he told me to pull a ring on the dashboard and hang on until until he said let go. I did, and of all the noise I ever heard, that car made it! I found out he had three self-made air horns under the hood. We pulled off on a detour road, and he pointed out a gallon jug sitting on a fence post and told me to grab it. It was a gallon of "white mule" which we promptly took back to the shop to sample. I was prepared for it to blow my hat off, but I have tasted rougher whiskey out of a liquor store. Of course all the fellows in the shop were watching me and expecting an explosion of some sort, so it was really one on them.

Steve shook his head and said, "I wouldn't have believed it if I hadn't seen it."

It was stout, but I didn't think it was bad at all.

One time Steve and George Cooley, a sheet metal worker, took me squirrel hunting. They told me to go one way, and they'd go another, and meet me up a draw farther on. I got a couple of squirrels on my way, and headed for the draw on an old tie-hacking road. (They made ties of hard wood by hand with axes at that time, and the men who made them were called, "tie-hackers.") I got to the draw on this old road, and there sat a fellow on the end of a log, with a rifle across his lap.

He said, "Ware y'all goin'?"

I said I was going up the draw to get some squirrels.

He drawled, "Big boy, you'ins ain't goin' up there, there ain't no squirrels. Better go back where y'all got them two."

I was wise to the fact that he was a still guard, but I wanted to see what he would have to say, so I told him I was going up there anyhow, to meet a couple of hunters.

He looked kind of scared, but said, "Y' ain't goin' any further. Who might y' be?"

I said Ed James, and he looked at me good and close, and then asked if I knew Steve James. When I told him Steve was my brother and I was going up to meet him, he grinned all over and shook hands with me.

"There's lots o' squirrels up thar. Take the left-hand branch of the creek and you can get a drink o' corn squeezins. But tell the fellows who you are sudden, they're a bit trigger happy."

Steve and George were there ahead of me, so no explanation was necessary.

My daughter Althaea got malaria and was in a bad way. The doctor didn't seem to do her any good, and I got worried so I went to his office to get to the bottom of it. He said he had done all he could for her, and I asked if getting her out of that country would help. He said that was about all that would help.

"In that case I'm leaving," I said.

That seemed to give him a jolt, he just couldn't believe I would quit my job and leave the country, or that we had three kids and had never lost any. I had seen many a little grave in people's back yards, but somehow it never hit me until I had sickness in my own family. He told me that people down there expect to lose at least one-third of their babies. I told him I was on my way.

CHAPTER 8

Back to Idaho

I bought a Model "T" pickup, put bows and canvas on it, and we were on our way to Idaho and fresh air. I went to Payette to see John Coats and find out if there was any work. I helped John and some of the farmers put up hay, then got a job picking apples. I got a little money ahead, and John interested me in buying some cows. I gave $25 a head for seven cows. Time wore on, and there was no such thing as a job. Winter was looking us in the face and those cows would have to be fed.

All the working people were out of jobs or on relief, and I couldn't see keeping those cows, so I sold them for $7 each. With half the money I bought some traps, and I found a fellow who wanted to kill a bear and who would haul me into the back country if I would guide him on a bear hunt, and he'd pay me $50 to boot. So I bought some grub, a few more traps, and three Siberian Husky work dogs. I gave my wife the $50 and what little was left of the cow money, and hit the trail for the back country. (The Mrs. told me afterwards that people said I had deserted my family and gone back to the mountains I had come from.)

We didn't get a bear, but he got a goat, and was the happiest dude I ever saw. I cached my grub and traps and hit for Monumental Creek, where I had heard Roy Eliot was living. I found him sitting in a carpet-bottom chair that sagged down until the seat was only a couple of inches from the floor.

I asked him, "What do you do during the long winters here?"

He said, "Set in this chair."

"What do you think about, here all alone?"

"Nothin'."

"I'm up against it, and I'm going to trap for a living this winter," I told him.

He grumbled, "Damn you, I was all set for a quiet winter and now you come along, and I suppose I'll ketch the disease and go bog snow and trap, too."

So he trapped the Rainbow Mountain country west of Monumental Creek, and I ran a line over Big Chief and Thunder Mountains. While I went back and got my grub and traps, he went out and got seven deer for our winter meat. We planned to meet at his place once a week if possible, and every two weeks for sure.

I cleared a little over $125 worth of furs a month and mailed them out to the Mrs. Money back where I was was just so much paper to bother with, and she could keep whatever she didn't need to spend. Roy and I both used skis. We made them out of lodgepole pines, eight foot three inches long, and fairly wide, for we were high up and the snow was like powder — and cold. I don't know how cold, but Roy's thermometer broke at forty below, and that was at his cabin, 2,000 feet below our traplines. When the sun came out it would shine clear and bright, but it was still just as cold, and the frost fell all day long.

Wolf, Husky and Spike were my dogs. Wolf was the mother of the other two. She was gray, and loved to work and loved to play — she knocked me flat many a time. She couldn't bark, but her throat would work and she'd look up at me and whine. Husky was red, a big powerful dog that could really pull, but she hated to work; she liked to be petted, but wasn't as playful as Wolf. Spike was chocolate colored and lived to work. He wasn't mean, but he preferred to be left alone. As soon as he was unhitched he would go off a ways and curl up in the snow. If I called he would come right up, but if I petted him he would turn his head and look away.

I trapped mostly marten, weasels (ermine) and some fox. One Saturday night I broke the curved end off one ski. It was a job to navigate with that blunt ski; I had to tie a cord to the end and pull on it to keep the end out of the snow. When I got in Roy had a good supper ready, and he said he would build me another ski the next day. I said that if there

were an old one around I would use that. I had a trap line I
needed to get to as I needed to send the furs to my family.
Besides, If a trapline is neglected wild animals will ruin the
pelts.

"You are an awful nuisance," Roy said, and he went outside. As I was doing the dishes I heard a tree fall. Roy cut
eight and one-half feet out of the best of it and hollered for
me to come help him lug it to the house. We brought it in,
and he started to whipsaw a skill block out of the middle of
it. He told me to hit the hay and get some rest. I woke up
early the next morning. Roy had stayed up all night, built a
big fire, built the ski, cured it, boiled the end, bent it back,
tied it, dried it out, doped it and built the harness and it was
ready to go. It took him all night, but from a live tree to a
finished ski in one night! It was probably the only one of its
kind ever built.

One morning I went to the mailbox, which was thirteen
miles from Roy's place, and there was a Montgomery Ward's
postcard with this message: "Your daughter Al had to have
an operation and is in no physical condition. Come out at
once."

There I was, in the dead of winter, with both Elk and
Warren Summits to ski over, and 150 miles to face. I figured
it was impossible, but I had to try. I had already skied
twenty miles that morning — eight miles from Thunder
Mountain to Roy's place (the Monumental Ranch) then thirteen miles to the mailbox. I had to go back to Roy's place,
thirteen miles, to get some furs, because I needed some
money to go out on. I left Spike and Wolf with Roy and took
Husky with me. I got the furs, went the thirteen miles back
to the mailbox, then it was two and one-half miles to Walt
Eastep's place down Big Creek. I sold the furs to Walt for
cash, and it was two and one-half miles back to the trail, and
I was on my way. Husky dragged the skis over Elk Summit,
as it was snowing so hard that I was bogging down. I didn't
have webs, but I wallowed through it. On the west side I
got to run a ways on skis down Elk Creek, and Husky didn't
catch up to me for several miles. I passed Warren Smith's
place just as it was coming dark; I crossed the South Fork
Bridge, where Tom Carry tried to get me to stop and sleep,

but I went on. Husky was pulling the skis again, as there wasn't enough snow to ski on. Halfway up Warren Summit I put on the boards (skis) tied a piece of gunny sack around them so I wouldn't slip backwards, and kept going. I was so tired that I had to stand and hold onto a tree now and then to keep from dropping down asleep. Of course if I had, I would have frozen to death.

Everyone thought I would fall down and freeze, but I fooled them. I was kept track of by phone after I crossed the South Fork. The grapevine in the back country was fast and reliable, and by then everybody knew about the message and my impossible journey. They phoned from Tom Carry's to Warren to Halfway House to McCall.

I ran into Earl Jacobsen (Ole) and he insisted on going on out with me. I had already been on the go all day and it was coming night, and I'd covered the better part of a hundred miles. Ole was half Dane and half German. I had met him while picking apples just after I came back from Arkansas. He was nineteen years old — a really good scout — I liked him. It was snowing so hard that the only way we could keep our direction was that the dense timber had been cut out for the road, and we would run into the trees and then work our way back to the road.

We passed Burgdorf, and all was dark. At Squaw Meadows Ole said, "Ed, I have had it. We have just got to stop here or they will find us when the snow thaws in the spring."

I told him to go on into Slim Fernard's and go to bed, but I was going on. He said if I could go on, he would too, and we kept those boards moving. We passed silently through the night, too tired even to talk; past the Halfway House, and finally came to the head of Payette Lake. From there the snow had been plowed through to McCall. We got a pole to hold between us and hooked a line to Husky, which made the going a little easier, as we could balance each other. At Lardo Billie Boydson told us that they were holding the train for me at McCall. We got to the train station at 8:00 A.M., after one day and one night on the trail. The crew asked me if Husky was gentle, I told them yes, they put her in the baggage car and told me to get aboard. Ole stayed in

McCall. They had rigged up two seats as a bed for me, fixed me a meal and gave me some moonshine. I ate a little, took a big shot of moon' and lay down. I didn't even know when the train pulled out, and it seemed I had just gotten to sleep when one of the crew woke me up at Payette.

I got Husky out of the baggage car and let her drag my skis, and went to the house where my family lived. The light was lit, and I could see through the window that the kids were at the table eating supper, and Althaea was right there with them. I found out Al had only had a tonsil operation, and my wife had telegraphed McCall that she was in good condition, that it was a minor operation, and that it was not necessary for me to come out. It was phoned to Warren, then phoned from there to the South Fork of the Salmon, and someone there wrote on the card the message which I received, which was just the opposite of the original message.

Of course I was glad Al was okay, but I hated the idea of that long trail back.

I had chained Husky to a tree in the front yard, and while I was eating supper a neighbor from across the street came over and said I had better put my dog somewhere else. He explained that he had a mean cat that attacked and rode every dog that came along, and he knew that my dog was tired after that trip and was afraid his cat would hurt her.

I told him, "You had better do something with your cat instead. That is no ordinary dog and she can take care of herself."

He said, "Well, I warned you to save trouble for that poor worn out dog." And he left, half mad, with a poor opinion of me for not taking care of my poor worn out dog.

Next morning we were wakened by a knocking at the door. There was the neighbor, and was he mad! He asked me to come outside, and there was Husky, still chained up, curled up sound asleep. Alongside of her lay half of a big black cat.

The neighbor said, "You will have to kill that dog. Its bad enough that she killed my cat, but to eat half of it. . . ." He started to sputter, "Well, I just won't stand for that!"

I said, "That's just too damn bad. Your cat jumped on my poor worn out, chained up dog."

I stayed one day and the next night, then caught a train for McCall and the long trail home. I knew I would have fur on the trapline that needed attention, and I needed the money for my family. It took me seven days to get back.

Back in the high country I never saw Wolf or Spike again. I heard rumors that Roy's brother was trapping coyotes and killed them. It was never proven to me, and I never saw Roy's brother, Ernest. In a way I was glad, because it would only have caused trouble and would not have brought my dogs back. The brother got terribly sick and died while they were trying to get him out to a doctor, and they buried him where he died. I have been within a hundred feet of the little knoll where his grave is, but I never thought enough of him to go see the spot.

I almost finished out the trapping season when placer gold was discovered on Smith Creek right in the elk grass roots. Roy and a fellow named Art Croswite staked claims just below the strike. The strike was sold out to a promoter who offered $5 a day plus grub, which was good money. I hired out to Bill Huten, superintendent of the Burns Hydraulic Mining Company. Ole came in too, and we were both stoneboaters all that summer. (Stoneboaters clean up bedrock and boulders after the sand, gravel and small rocks are washed into the sluice box and on down river.) Roy and Croswite sold their claims to the company, retained a royalty on the output, and also went to work for them.

Bill Huten had to leave for a spell, and he put me in charge of the clean-up and division of gold. Croswite thought he was a big shot while Bill was gone, and he made things tough for Ole. He called Ole a big, dumb Swede and they locked horns. Ole climbed out of the pit and went after Croswite, who grabbed double-bitted axe and started swinging. Ole took the axe away from him, threw it aside and shoved Croswite into the pit, which had about sixteen inches of water in the bottom. Ole pushed Croswite's face under and began to punch hell out of him, and he sure made the water fly — he was putting all he had into it. Ole was nineteen and weighed about two hundred. Some of us jumped in after them, and I got Ole off Croswite, who was plenty beat up and about two-thirds drowned. Not that I cared, but Ole would have gotten in trouble if he'd killed him; there were too many witnesses.

When Bill came back he told us that the mine wasn't paying and they would soon close out the jobs. Ole stayed the last month, but I went back to my family in Payette. There just wasn't any work, and those who were working were getting $1.50 a day and the work was only seasonal. We moved to Sandpoint where there were some big saw-mills running, but there were two men for every job, and they were only paying $2 for ten hours work. I finally got a job on the Spokane International Railroad on the section gang. I worked with every nationality but my own, under an Austrian who could barely speak English. I made $85 a month, and a lot of the neighbors looked down on me for it, but I fed my family. Ole was out of work and came and stayed with us most of the winter, then finally found a job in a restaurant in Wallace. I got laid off in the spring. The Austrian told me it was just a layoff, but the next day there was another Austrian in my place.

Then I went to work at the Arctic Fur Farm, run by a foxy farmer who was running a skin game. He made money, but the company didn't. I worked there a long time, learned the business and built up a herd of silver foxes of my own. I couldn't stay because of family trouble. The Mrs. never was the same after we came out of the back country. She was a big city girl, and I was just what I was.

I had $600 in the bank, and as the banks were going broke all around, I decided to draw mine out, and got told by my wife how dumb I was, so we went around and around over it for a few days. Finally without saying anything to her, I went down to the bank, wrote out a check for the full amount and presented it to the cashier. He went and showed it to the head mogul who came and tried to talk me out of withdrawing it. The more he talked, the more determined I was to get my money.

It was after 11 A.M., and I told him, "I have heard all I want, I want my money now, or I will drag you right through your little window."

He said, "Its so close to noon, why don't you go get some lunch and think it over?"

"I'm through thinking, and I want my money before either one of us leaves here."

He finally went and got the money, slammed it down on the counter, and I grabbed it up and left. The bank closed up for lunch and never opened its doors again.

I took the money home, turned it over to the Mrs. got a bawling out for drawing it out, and never saw it again. I had had all I could take, so I just left the country and everything in it. Ole had bought half interest in my foxes, and I just left the other half and lit out. I wound up in Klamath Falls, Oregon with two cents and a wedding ring in my pocket. I took them out and threw them just as far as I could.

Soon Ole joined me in Klamath Falls, and he said, "We'll just start all over and build up a herd — half the foxes are still yours."

I dealt for a ranch six miles south of Chemult, and in a few years we built up a good herd of foxes. Then Ole wanted to quit and go the Coquille where his folks lived, so we split the foxes and he pulled out. My son, Ed, came down and wanted to go into the business with me. I turned half interest over to him. Of course he had been raised around foxes.

I decided to go to the back country for a visit, and while I was back there I heard that there was a new party on Whimstick Creek by the name of Elkins. Sure enough, it was old Howard himself! He had sold out to Dick Green and moved to Whimstick Creek to be a big game guide and outfitter. I visited with him for a few days, then I had to get back to help my son with the foxes.

About a year later it came over the radio that the Japs had bombed Pearl Harbor. Ed turned to me and said, "Dad, I'm going."

I asked him when, and he said, "In the morning."

He was gone until after the Second World War, and he came back a Bosuns Mate 1st Class, and got married.

That summer Howard came out from the back country and said to me, "Ed, I have come out to take you back where you belong."

As a fur farmer, Miller Creek Ranch, Chemult, Oregon in the late '30s

I deeded the ranch over to my son, Ed, and got ready to go back with Howard. I had worked for the state the last five years, running everything from a wheelbarrow to a snow-go (or rotary). I took out my driver's and chauffeur's licenses, tore them up, and swore I would never drive another car.

I was all ready to go when Ed asked me, "Dad, what'll I do with Tamarack?"

By all means shoot him before he kills someone."

Tamarack was a desert horse I had bought for fox feed, but he was such a fine animal that I broke him out, and he was one of the best horses that I ever saw. But he was strictly a one man horse. I could do anything with him, and while he didn't like anyone else, he would tolerate them as long as I was there. But if I wasn't there he would kick, strike or bite and try to kill anyone else.

When I went back with Howard I was around fifty, and I made up my mind that I would finish out my life in the back country. I did not know that I had long years ahead of me — some of them good, some not so good, some hell.

CHAPTER 9

Home to the Back Country —
For Good?

We took a plane from McCall, and Jim Larkin flew us in. Both he and Bob Fogg were top pilots, but I came close to getting my everlasting with both of them. I'm out of my element in a plane, and while I've done quite a bit of back country flying, I hope I'll never have to fly again. The top deck of a high bucking horse is about as high as I ever should have gone.

We landed at Whimstick Creek Ranch, which belonged to Howard. He had bought the ranch for $1000 from Wallace Beery when Beery and Gloria Swanson separated. Wallace had given Raleigh Campbell $500 for it; Raleigh had paid $35 for tax and title. The original owner had been Jess Root, who had bet the government $36 against 160 acres that he could homestead it, and he won. But the Salmon River claimed Jess. He was last seen by Frank Lantz, floating in a whirlpool, long past help. Anyway, Howard eventually sold that same ranch for $27,000. Later he went out and got himself a wife who shot him in the back of the head. I don't know what happened to her. Howard was a tough egg, but he deserved a lot better than that.

I stayed with Howard at his ranch for awhile, then went to Chamberlain Basin to see George McCoy, another real friend of mine. He had a bunch of cattle on the Stonebreaker Ranch, and he talked me into wintering with him. We took turns feeding cattle and hunting cougar with dogs. A man can wear his legs off clear up to the knees hunting cougar, and a week at a time was usually all we could do before we had to trade back to feeding cattle.

The cougar hounds needed to be changed every three or four days. A good hound just won't quit, he'll run cougar until his feet are so sore that he leaves blood in his tracks. I have put buckskin moccasins on hounds, but that won't

Root Ranch, once owned by Wallace Beery

work when they're running a hot trail. A top cougar hound is beyond price. The best ones we had were crossbred Black and Tans, Redbones and a little Walker. Too much Walker blood and they were inclined to chase deer, in which case we had to shoot them before they ruined the other dogs. A good dog is a specialist, and only runs cougar. We also used a little bloodhound breeding, which tends to slow them down, but it improves their noses. The Platt hounds had too much nerve and would fight when they should just bay the big cats, and they soon got killed.

One time George and I decided to go scout around together for cougar, so we got our skis and headed for the Main Salmon River. The snow was about a foot deep with a light crust. We came to a place where there was no brush or lodge poles, and it was a good half mile down to the Salmon. It is a big, swift-running river, and certain death if you hit it that time of year. It is all white water, frozen over in places into ice bridges; slush ice forms on the rocks, thaws and

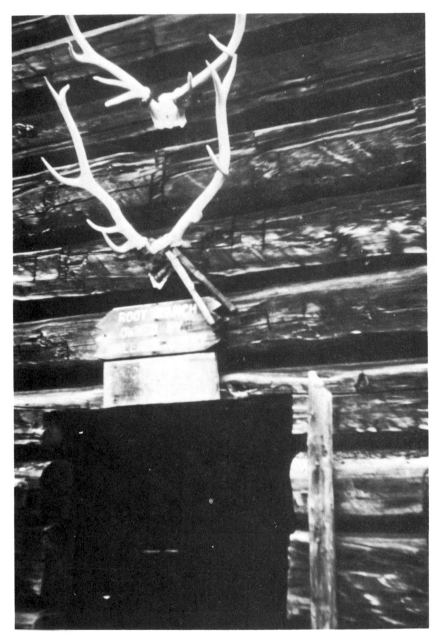

At the Root Ranch

Ed James in 1950

jams up ahead of riffles. The water backs up until it breaks it up and the whole mass goes over. Sometimes up to twenty or thirty feet high. It breaks up into chunks maybe ten to twelve feet square; they wash down, lodge in rocks and pile up. The water escaping under and around these chunks splashes and freezes, forming ice bridges that you can cross on if you've got the guts, or don't have the sense to stay off them. So George and I had come to this steep, open snow covered slope, about a quarter of a mile across.

It didn't look good to me, and I told George, "I haven't lost any cougar down in this country. We really don't need to cross here."

He said, "Hell, Jess." (He always called me that, damn him. I never liked it.) "Come on!"

He took off, I tested the snow and it seemed okay, so I followed him. I was relieved when we got across, I could think of a lot of more pleasant ways to kick the bucket besides that icy water. We got to the timber and were safe, as you can always stop yourself from sliding in timber or brush. George found an ice bridge and we crossed the river to the Nez Perce side. We were far below any trails, in what was called "impassable" country. But to the so-called natives, none of it was impassable. We followed the river down aways, then came to a big, flat rock, probably fifty feet across, which sloped down steeply, then dropped off into the river. There was about eight inches of frozen snow on it. We climbed up aways, then George said, "Hell, I'm going to cross here."

"I expect to take some chances in this country," I said, "but you are plumb loco to try this. We can find a better crossing somewhere else."

"Aw, Jess, this'll be like shooting fish on a riffle," George said.

And he started across that sheet of ice. About ten feet out he started to slip sideways, slowly but surely. He tried to slide toward me, but only succeeded in slipping faster. I stuck my skis in the snow and moved down beside the rock to help if I possibly could. We had packed cargo ropes, three-eighths of an inch thick and twenty-two feet long, but by the time I got a loop in my rope I didn't have enough slack to reach him. Just below him was a much steeper slope, and we knew if he got that far, it would be "Katy, close the gate" for him. He kept sliding toward that sickening drop off; it was like watching a horror film in slow motion, and I was helpless to do anything. He figured there was no help, and neither did I.

He called, "So long, Jess, this is one time you had more sense than me!"

About twelve feet above the drop off was a little sprig of mountain mahogany sticking up through the snow, about eighteen inches long and the thickness of a lead pencil. We both saw it at the same time. He slid to it, caught it and eased himself by so his skis wouldn't hit it. This was his only chance, or it would surely be good-bye. George weighed around 190, but mahogany is tough, and it stopped him. I rendered my loop and after a couple of tries he caught the extreme end of my rope.

He said, "Don't try to pull. Just bog down as deep as you can with your heels, sit down and hold on."

We got the rope tight, and I said, "Try it. I'll hold you or we will both go!"

He hollered, "To hell with you, if I start to slip, turn me loose."

I cussed at him and told him to quit talking and try it. He let the mahogany gradually slip through his fingers, slid down a little, then around and off the rock into the snow!

He sat there quietly for a moment, then said, "This is a hell of a lot better than a ducking in that river! Let's go up to Frank Lantz's and have a couple of drinks and hole up with him for the night. We'll let those cats be for now."

It sorta gives me the creeps when I really think about it, even after all these years. And to think that in a few years George was crippled up in a car wreck outside, where it is supposedly safe and civilized. He only lived a couple of years after the wreck.

We got a few cougar between us, then George got word that his mother was ill, so he took his cat hides and left me to feed the cattle. That stopped the cougar hunting. He didn't come back until spring.

I remember sitting in the living room one morning after

feeding. It was thirty-three below zero. Along came three moose — two cows and a calf. Those old cows would strad-dle a quaking aspen tree and walk up it until it was bent to the snow, then all three of them would eat the tops out of it down to branches the size of your thumb, then go on up country in search of more aspens. The elk and deer were miles below, pawing out bunch grass.

I turned the stock loose down the country and grabbed a plane for McCall. I figured it was about time to paint the town a little. I went into a bar owned by Brad Carry (Tom's brother). Brad got glasses for both of us and we had a snort.

About that time George came in and said, "I heard you were in town, and I knew you would need some help to do this drinking right. You never could do anything alone!"

We had a few drinks, and Brad was kind of ornery — he wouldn't let us pay for anything. Just when we had our glas-ses licked he would fill them up again. We were taking it slow and peddling a lot of wa-hi when some bird came in and sat next to us. He didn't say anything and didn't order a drink, but just sat and watched us. After he left, I turned to George and asked, "Was that bird looking for you or me?"

"He didn't say. Don't let it bother you. My brothers al-ways spoil these towns for me." (George and his brothers had been known to take a few places apart.)

I asked Brad who the fellow was, and he said, "He's the new town clown. George, he probably heard you were in town and wanted to get a look at you."

Two women came in, and one of them was on the heavy side. They ordered drinks, and the heavy one complained that the stool was too close to the bar for her. George told her to get up, then he grabbed the stool by the top, gave it a jerk that pulled the screws out of the floor, and set it back aways. She said that was much better.

George asked, "Brad, how much extra for the stool?"

Brad said, "Hell, that's okay; we've got to make the ladies comfortable."

George had a pinto horse that he wanted me to break. He couldn't break horses to be gentle, he was just too rough with them. I tried to buy this pinto, but George told me that if I wanted him, just take him. I offered him $150, but he

Ed James with pack string

said that horse wasn't worth the money. I wouldn't take it
without paying, but I went ahead and broke him. He was a
bucker, and would buck himself off his feet. He fell with me
four times, the last time he fell into a stake and rail fence
and scattered it all over. George told me to kill the damn
thing before it killed me, but I rode the pinto all summer
pulling pack string for the forest service. I tried again to buy
him, and offered George $250, but he said I was loco, to just
take the horse. I was just as stubborn as he was, so George
kept the horse. It wasn't ridden that winter, and I warned
George that it would probably buck when he rode it in the
spring. There was this fellow who was supposed to be an
expert rider, and he told George that he would spur the
bucking out of the pinto. (I never saw that done successfully
with a horse, but it works with mules.) The expert couldn't
keep company with the horse at all. Unfortunately, the horse
got to playing and hit a hay mower that some dumb ape had

left sitting with the sickle bar up, and he had to be destroyed. So I didn't get the horse, and George didn't get any good out it either.

That fall I was coming up Chamberlain Creek with the government's string of "hardtails" (mules) and I met George riding with a dude. They had been hunting and had killed an elk. George never cargoed or "mantied" up meat, he just quartered it with the hair still on, and packed it hair side next to the bell mare with the meat exposed to the brush and rock. He was really an expert packer, but he just didn't have much use for most dudes. Anyway, George pulled up off the trail with his saddle horse, bell mare and pack mule and the dude to let me by with the big pack string.

When he pulled even with me he stopped to talk. "What do you think of my 'pet,' Ed?"

He meant his mule. I had heard about that particular hardtail. It had a bad name, and looked like it deserved it . Anytime George heard of any ornery critter, he couldn't rest until he got it, and he was especially proud of that mule. Of course you couldn't pack that animal like other mules, you had to snub it up close and work over the bell mare, and that mule would run anyone out of a corral. She was just as ugly as her disposition; her nose wasn't just roman, her whole head was bowed.

I answered, "If she was mine, I'd feed her to the coyotes."

About that time she began to slip downhill, and she had to climb hard to get up beside the bell mare. She looked at the warm elk meat, grabbed into it and started to grind it with her teeth. It wasn't a very nice sight, and the dude didn't seem to like seeing that mule bite chunks out of his elk, so I pulled on so they could get back on the trail.

About three weeks later I came back to the Chamberlain Ranger Station, and although I had a permanent camp there, I always went over to George's place, (the Stonebreaker Ranch). Gill McCoy, George's brother, was the ranger there. At the station Blanch, Gill's wife, phoned George and told him that I had come in. In a few minutes he showed up, and I asked him, "How are you making it with that elk-eating mule?"

A pack string leaving Chamberlain Basin Ranger Station, 1951

"She's tame as a kitten. I can go right into the corral and halter her now."

I said, "Go tell that to your dudes."

Blanch fed us, then we rode over to George's place, and there in the corral was that bow-headed mule.

I laughed, "Go get your halter and put it on your pet."

He got a halter, climbed over the fence and ordered the mule to come to him. She came out to the middle of the corral and stood there with her ears laid flat, grinding her teeth and wringing her tail. George walked up and put the halter on her, and led her over and tied her up.

I said, "I see it, but I still don't believe it."

"Hell, Jess, its plumb easy when you know how. You are a wonder with wild horses, but you don't know your hard-tails. Its simple. All you've got to do is learn how to be meaner than they are. You'll learn that after you're around them awhile."

I guess I'm dumb, but I never learned, or cared to learn.

That fall George and I trailed beef out of the back country. He got into a poker game and bet his cattle, and won the whole joint: bar, restaurant, grocery store and some $800 in cash. The next morning he asked me if I would run the places for him. I told him I wanted no part of it. He dug in his pocket, got out all the IOU's from the game and tore them up. I asked him why.

"Jess, if you had wanted to work them it would have been okay, but I don't know nothin' about such stuff. We'll keep the $800, we might take a notion to paint McCall, but those fellows I won from have wives and kids to fetch up and feed; we don't need their junk."

CHAPTER 10

The Pinto Dude Ranch

Later that fall I got a job wrangling dudes and guiding big game hunters at the Pinto Dude Ranch on Cabin Creek (a tributary of Big Creek) for Joe and Carol Maby. Bless her heart, Carol was as wonderful a person as Joe was no good, and that is saying a lot. Joe and Dewey Moore, up on the old Rouston place, were feuding at the time. Dewey had a reputation for being a trouble maker — he just loved to see people in a scrap, and I learned that Joe was more or less that same breed. One night I came in after dark and hammered at Joe's door, and disguising my voice, I hollered that I was Dewey Moore. Carol came to the door, and when she saw it was me she got a big bang out of it. She said Joe had hightailed it for the bedroom when I had hollered. Then she burst out laughing and Joe came out with a lopsided grin on his face, claiming he knew it was me all along.

Several days later I was going past Dewey's place and he asked me to stay for supper.

He asked me, "Have you heard that Joe offered $500 in Boise for someone to kill me?"

"No, and I don't believe that Joe would do that." I answered, and when he asked me why, I said, "With all his faults, you will have to admit that Joe has a good business head on him." Dewey admitted that, and I continued, "He wouldn't offer $500 to get you killed. Joe knows I would do the job for less than that!" Neither one of them ever tried to get me to speak against the other again. I wrangled dudes for Joe for two years, and later married Dewey's daughter.

Carol told me a story about George and Joe that I got a kick out of: George had a couple of pinto yearlings, and his brother's mother-in-law (who had no business doing so) sold them to Joe for $50 apiece. George heard about it and rode over to the Pinto Dude Ranch to get his yearlings. They were friends, but no one stole anything from George without having him on their tail. When he rode up, Joe told him, "Get off and come eat with us."

George said, "I came on business, and that business is to get my yearlings."

Joe said, "I bought those yearlings, and I'm going to keep them."

"Joe, you know me better than that. When I say something, I do it."

Joe said, "If you take those yearlings, it will be over my dead body."

"If it comes to that, I'll do that, too." George said.

Joe said, "Come on in and we'll talk about it over a drink."

"There's nothing to talk over," George told him, "but as a friend I'll have that drink with you."

Joe began to hedge, because he knew when he bought those colts it wasn't an honest deal. "If you'll make good that $50 each, you can take the colts."

"That's not the point," George insists. "They are my yearlings, and you knew you were buying stolen colts, and that is that. You will just have to take the money out of the old lady's hide. They're not worth $50, but that's your tough luck."

Carol spoke up. "Joe, quit arguing about it. They're George's property."

Joe couldn't see it that way, but suggested, "I have a couple of fifths. Lets forget the yearlings and kill the fifths."

George said, "That's okay with me, but I have to get back to Chamberlain and it will be a long drag pulling a couple of half broke yearlings, so I'll want to get away early in the morning."

Carol took Joe aside, "Tomorrow morning, you tell George to take those colts, because they are his. Besides, he will take them anyway."

So next morning they had breakfast, and then when they got up from the table Joe said, "George, you can take those colts without anymore trouble."

George replied, "Joe, you know that's the smart thing to

do. We've been friends a long time, and I'd hate like hell to have to kill you to get those colts."

Joe said, "Let's shake on it."

They shook hands, and George said, "You know damn well I wouldn't let you or anyone else steal a horse from me. You keep them, but I'd see you in hell before I'd let you steal them."

A couple of years later I broke those two colts for Joe. They were okay, but they weren't worth fighting over.

The weather was mild at the first of elk season, and that's bad because the elk stay scattered in the high country and are hard to hunt. Our hunters did fairly well. One time three dudes landed, two Lithuanians and one Jew. One of the Lithuanians said, "Shake hands with Pajama Joe — you will soon find out why he's called that. And this big fellow here is a Jew, but a good Jew."

The Jew was crippled in one knee from a football injury, and he stayed at the lodge. One fellow hunted alone, and Pajama Joe hired me as a special guide. They were all multimillionaires, and all really good sports, and they didn't kick about anything. (Joe got his nickname from the expensive silk pajamas he always lounged around in.) I had Pajama Joe out for five days and we didn't see an elk and I was getting pretty discouraged, but Joe said, "Don't let it bother you, I'm having the time of my life. Besides, I need to knock a little of this belly off."

On the last day Carol packed us a lunch and we hit for what was known as the "Big Hole" — a high, deep basin, where I thought there could be a few elk. As we got up toward the basin, there was a little snow. I told Joe I would hang our lunch on a limb, and we could get it on our way back. He didn't say anything, but he looked at me as if he thought I was some kind of a nut. We moved on, and found a bull elk's tracks, and two cows. It was steep country, and Joe just couldn't go very far without having to sit down and rest, I knew the elk were traveling faster than we were.

Joe asked me, "How much farther to the top?"

About three-fourths of a mile," I replied. "Then we'll come to the basin, where the elk might bed down and give us a chance to catch up."

Joe said, "Ed, I just can't make it. Why don't you go on alone, if you can find your way back to me?"

"Don't worry about that, I'm home here."

I lit out in a dog trot to make up some time, and when I got to the top of the ridge I found that the elk had not stopped, but had gone straight on across. I turned back, and found Joe just here I had left him. I wouldn't have left most dudes alone that way, as they get ideas and start wandering around and get lost. But Joe wasn't like that. He knew he'd get lost, and wanted no part of it. He told me sit down and rest, but I said I wasn't tired.

He said, "I saw you run up that hill, and I don't see how any man could do that. But I figured out one thing, Ed, you would be damn tough eating!"

We went back down aways, and I mentioned that I was getting a bit gaunted up, and asked Joe if he could eat some lunch.

"I sure could, but how in hell can we find that lunch hanging in one certain tree? There must be a million trees and they all look alike. We'd better hit for the lodge before we starve."

We went on a couple of hundred feet, and I reached up and untied the lunch, sat down on a log and told him to come on and eat.

He just stood there and looked at me, then said, "Ed, we came back from a different direction, and you went straight to that lunch. I saw you do it or I wouldn't have believed it."

I told him again, "I'm home here. If we were back in New York, I couldn't find my hip pocket with both hands."

He just couldn't get over my finding that lunch, and back at the lodge he had to tell everyone all about it.

Pajama Joe and the other two dudes were due to leave the next day, so Carol radioed out for a plane. Jim Larkin landed early next morning, then was socked in by fog.

Jim said, "My mother wanted me to get her some elk meat, and this is as good a time as any. Grab a gun, Ed. Maybe one of us can get a cow for Ma."

Pajama Joe said, "It's hopeless. Ed and I tramped a

On the trail, 1951

thousand miles and didn't even see one; there just ain't any elk."

We got out guns anyway, and going up Cow Creek I told Jim how slim the hunting had been. Cow Creek forked, one fork went to Black Butte, and one to a high saddle going over the Big Hole. Jim took the Black Butte fork, and I took the other. We weren't likely to see each other until we got back to the lodge. I was almost at the saddle when I heard elk running. I saw the last of them go over the saddle, then a two-year-old cow came trotting behind. I took careful aim and laid her down. I gutted her out, and propped her belly cavity open with a stick so she would cool, and covered her up with brush. Then I headed back for the lodge. I felt pretty good. At least the dudes would know there was elk in the country, and the Larkins would have meat. In a couple of miles I came across a spike bull, and killed him with one easy shot, cleaned him and left him to cool. Back at the lodge Jim was already there, and the dudes were all excited. They told me Jim had connected on elk. Jim and I packed the meat in the next morning, and the following day the fog lifted and Jim flew the three dudes out. They were good dudes, and most of them are; but each year I would run into some that made me swear to never take another dude out.

We had three dudes come in from Bakersfield. If they ever read this, and I hope they do, they will remember Rush Point. I took them over to Cave Creek to get deer. (The limit was two each.) They did more shooting than I like to see, but they got four or five deer, and were more than satisfied. When we got back to the lodge, the plane was in from McCall. I don't remember if it was Jim Larkin or Bob Fogg, but the pilot told us that he had spotted a bunch of elk bedded down, and told me where. The dudes got all excited and asked me if we could go after them in the morning. I told them that I would have to go after the deer they had shot that day. They said to hell with them, we can always get deer. Of course I went and packed in the deer meat, and they were pretty put out about it. When I got back they were shooting at deer up on Horse Mountain, and I had to go put a stop to that. I unloaded the meat, got a fresh horse, and went up where they were shooting. I found one deer with a broken leg, and one that was gut-shot. I killed them both and hung them the best I could. I went back the next morning and got the mess, and those dudes tried to refuse to put their tags on them. They said that they had not really been after meat — they were just "having a little fun and trying out their guns." Of course we guides advertised those kinds of dudes, and they were unable to get anyone to take them out the next year.

There were four doctor dudes due to fly in soon, and I had been out scouting around trying to locate some elk. I had gotten in late the night before, and again this evening and I was plenty tired. When I came in Joe told me I had to turn around and go back out. Those three dudes were up on Rush Point with no grub. He had taken them up there that afternoon.

I asked him, "Why in hell didn't you pack grub with you when you took them up there?"

He didn't answer me, so Carol spoke up. "Ed, you've been going day and night, and you're not going up there tonight. It's too dangerous. Joe and those dudes were lit up when they left here, and they took plenty of whiskey with them. You just forget them and go get some rest."

Joe was sobering up by this time, and he confessed that they were all pretty well loaded when they had left, and they had neglected to take any food or blankets with them. I was darned tired and not a little disgusted, but I couldn't leave them to freeze all night. So with a sigh, I turned and went back out, took a saddle horse and loaded some grub and supplies on two pack horses. It was dark and the trail was slippery. I found the dudes, all right. They had a little fire going inside the tent, and of course it was full of smoke. Two of them had on low topped shoes. They had scraped the snow off the ground inside the tent, so all the fire did was make the floor muddy. They were a sorry looking lot. I took down the tent, packed it and their guns up and told them to hit the trail ahead of me on foot. It was a steep, narrow trail, and the horses had not improved it coming up. One of my pack horses went over, and slid into some lodge pole pines, or I would have lost her. I got back on the trail, and went back to herding the dudes. I could hear them slip and fall now and then, and it kind of did my heart good.

When we got back to the lodge I woke Joe up and told him to go take care of his dudes, that I was through with dudes and big game outfitting. I went out to my shack to get some sleep, but Carol came and woke me up and talked me into staying. The next day the four doctor dudes flew in, and I took them out and spot camped them. When I got back Joe tried to talk me out of leaving, and I finally agreed.

"Joe, I'll stay only on these conditions: You never take another dude out, never have anything to say about anything, and let Carol run the business end of things. I will take care of the dudes, and I want a helper."

I got my helper, Bill Sullivan — a good packer and guide, if you could keep the bottles hidden. Carol said she would take care of that, and from then on her word was law.

Carol and Joe wanted me to winter with them, but I went out to Klamath Marsh instead, and worked feeding cattle for a Klamath Indian named Hugh Night. I broke a few horses and had a pretty good winter. If you have a little Indian blood you are accepted, and I never lived around a happier people.

The following spring I phoned into McCall to see if I could get a job with the forest service, and Jim Hackiday, the assistant supervisor, said, "Ed, if we didn't have an opening we'd make one for you."

In McCall, Jim told me that Gill McCoy, George's brother, was about to go down the Salmon to winter range, gather up all the Payette National Forest stock, shoe them, distribute the local stock, and take the back country stock in for the summer.

We found all the stock — 143 head of horses and mules — except for a big bay mule named Monty, which had been in my string before. He was the only mule in my lifetime that I ever liked. He was more like a horse than a mule, you didn't have to drag him, and you could trust him. We found where he had slipped and rolled off the mountain. It wouldn't have hurt my feelings to see some of the others get killed, but old Monty was a real loss. We got them all shod, and started for McCall. It took us eleven days to make the

Government pack string of mules on Big Creek trail

trip, and there was only one day when it didn't rain or sleet on us — that of course was the day we got into McCall.

Then we headed for Landmark and got rained and snowed on some more. Dan Levan was driving pickup and tending camp for us. It sure was handy to come into a camp already set up for us. Dan was a top cook and a prince of a fellow. He was district ranger of Big Creek and Chamberlain. Gill McCoy was the Chamberlain ranger, and "Skuke" McCoy, Gill and George's brother, was alternate ranger at Big Creek. Skuke was short for "skukem" — Indian for "big." Skuke was a small man. I did not know another name for him, though I guess he had one. They just don't come any better than Skuke. I was just the packer and Dan was really over us all, but you never would have known it if you had been around us. I remember when we got to Landmark; it was the coldest spot in the United States that day, according to the weather report.

We had four bronco mules that were only broke to lead

— they were young and everything licked them. One of them got chased off the road and fell down a steep grade. There was about three feet of snow, and the road was just a bulldozed track that had been cleared for us. Gill said we would just have to shoot the mule, Dan drove up and he agreed that there was no way to get that mule back up on the road, if we tried, it would just slide further down the mountainside. I was riding a big blue buckskin that belonged to Mary Henson. She was the lookout on Acorn Butte and had wanted me to bring the horse in for her. I had fifty feet of rope on my saddle and just the width of the road to pull on, and I don't suppose the horse had ever been roped off before. But I tossed my rope and got it around the mule's neck. It started to struggle and the horse got scared and pulled back to keep from being dragged off the road. I kept my turns and up came the hardtail onto the road. It just lay there, and Dan said, "We might just as well have shot it when it was still down there. Why in hell didn't you stop when I yelled? Its head and front end were clear under the snow and you plowed a trench mule wide and deep and choked him besides!"

I said, "I couldn't have stopped if I'd wanted to. If this horse had started bucking we would have had two animals down there and Mary would have never forgiven me."

"I thought you had a reason." Dan said.

Gill was fooling around the mule and called for more slack on the rope. He pulled the loop off the mule, gave it a kick in the backside, and the mule jumped up, started to bray and ran back into the bunch. After that, that mule couldn't be made to get near the outer edge of the road.

When we got to Yellow Pine we left the pickup. Dan saddled a horse, and we packed our gear on six Decker pack rigs, but there wasn't enough room for my bed and stuff. So I rolled it all up and cargoed it in several manties, then we caught one of the wild unbroken mules and "siwashed" it on him. We snubbed him up, threw my cargo over his back, cinched it down tight, put another cinch around his breast, tied it tightly to the ropes that held my bed, put another cinch around his backside and turned him loose. He jumped around and bumped into some of the other mules, but they

Typical pack rigging

kicked and bit him until he quit. We headed for Monumental Summit in a cold drizzle which soon turned to snow. The old horses and mules knew where they were going and wanted to get there. The snow was about four feet deep at the summit, but they would rear up and lunge ahead, and when one got winded another would take its place breaking trail. Dan and Gill were riding ahead, and Skuke and I were bringing up the drag. At Roosevelt Lake it was getting dark, and was cold and wet with about three feet of snow. The Monumental Ranch was about six miles below the lake; it was deserted, but we knew there was shelter and feed for the stock there. All of a sudden the stock began to bunch up and Dan called back that there was a snow slide across the trail, and no way around. With a mountain on one side and Monumental Creek on the other, our only choice was to cross the creek.

It was too dark to see each other but Gill hollered, "Ed, if we can get across we can make it to the ranch. I don't know how deep it is, but its only about fifty feet across."

I called back, "Hit 'er, Gill, I can't be much wetter and colder than I am now, and there is no place here to camp."

Dan yelled, "You damn fools will drown."

I replied, "We can't drown but once!"

Dan yelled stop, but I heard one splash after another, then Gill called out, "Come on in, the water's fine! But Ed, your new hardtail went under, bed and all."

Dan hollered, "Get the hell out of there before you freeze."

Skuke was on a horse he knew, and jumped him off into the water, went down to his horse's head, then swam a little ways and waded out. I knew nothing about my horse, but he didn't want to be left behind, so he slid down into the water up to the top of my saddle and swam high, and soon we caught up with the drag — only they were not dragging. They wanted to get out of there as much as we did.

We got to the ranch, caught the pack stock, roped the mule with my bed on him, pulled my bed off and turned him loose. Dan could hardly talk, and he was shaking like a fence wire in a blizzard.

Gill told him, "Go inside and try to build a fire. You're no help to us out here the way you're shaking."

Dan dropped his bridle reins and left us, then in a few minutes he came back out and asked me where my bed was. I told him, and asked why he wanted it.

"Ed, I saw you roll up a fifth in your bed. You have broken every rule in the blue book, and you will get us all canned one of these days, but I was plumb glad when I saw you do that. I should have thought of it myself, but the liquor store wasn't open. Where's that fifth?"

"You're wrong about that, Dan," I said. "I rolled up two fifths."

He grabbed my bed and high-tailed it back in the house. We just got the last horse unloaded and turned loose when Dan came out. He had killed half a fifth and the only effect it had was that he'd quit shaking. He said later that he honestly believed he would have died that night if he hadn't had that drink. After we killed the other half of the bottle, Gill went to get the other fifth and found that my bed was dry. I had cargoed it so tightly and used so many manties that the water hadn't penetrated to my bed. I was the only one that night who didn't have to stay up and dry his bed.

Skuke said, "Its a good thing you had those two fifths, or we would have ganged up on you and taken your bed away from you, but chances are you saved all our hides with that whiskey."

Its not likely that I saved anyone, you can go through a lot in the country if you don't pack in germs with you. But you always caught it when the dudes came in, as you are not immune to cold germs and they sure latch onto you when someone brings them in from outside.

I was disappointed when I got back to Big Creek headquarters. Dan told me they were going to discontinue the big strings of pack mules, and would only be taking a bell mare and two or three mules to fetch in the smoke jumpers. From then on most of equipment would be dropped by parachute. My job would be to run a trail crew, and just take enough pack stock to carry their equipment. I didn't especially like that, but I had no choice. We left a lot of the stock at headquarters with Dan and Skuke, and Gill and I headed for Grass Mountain guard station where we stayed overnight with Wilmer Shaver, a fire guard.

I remember the next morning there were over three hundred elk on the meadows. That wasn't surprising since there were lots of elk back there then; also whitetail deer, moose and mule deer by the droves. We started for Whimstick Ranch, and on the way we saw a plane circling and stopped to watch it.

Gill said, "Ed, there is your trail crew coming in. Lets go meet them. Then why don't you go down to McCalley Creek and make camp and give me a chance to get acquainted with them."

We went on down and said howdy and shot the bull a little, then I said I'd better go make camp. As I started to pull out I called back to Gill, "What do you want for supper?"

"Rattlesnake" was the answer.

"If I fry rattlesnake, you all have to eat it."

It was really rattlesnake country in the lower breaks. I set up camp and fixed supper for the boys, but I didn't have time that night to get a snake.

Next morning Gill said, "Let's take the trail grader and grade the trail to Grass Mountain and I'll have the crew go up Chamberlain and clean out the trail there, and we will all come back here for supper. You don't have a grader hardtail in your string, but there's a young mule that should be good to train."

We got the mule, put the harness on him, hooked the tugs to the grader, and Gill said, "I'll do the grading, and you hang onto the mule."

That suited me, as I had visions of what hanging onto those handles in those rocks behind that big wild mule would be like. I was right — Gill hit the rocks and the grader would bounce, and that mule made Gill run high, wide and handsome. When we got to the top we stopped to eat, and hung a nose bag on the mule.

Gill said, "We didn't do much grading, but we loosened a thousand rocks. Maybe we can knock a few of them off the trail on the way back."

I hung the nose bag on the mule's harness hame and we

Ed James in white hat helping smoke jumpers unload at Chamberlain Ranger Station. Plane was one of the last of the old Ford tri-motors.

started back. Then I spotted a really big rattlesnake going down ahead of us. I yelled, "Stop everything, here is an eating size snake!"

I tied up and went after the snake, which crawled under a flat rock that hung out over the trail, and coiled up. Gill brought me a green forked stick and I eased it around the snake's neck and pushed it hard into the dirt. I reached in and caught it just back of the head, pulled it out, went over to a log and cut its head off so it couldn't bite itself or us, then stuffed the snake into the feed bag on the mule. We didn't get much grading done on the way back. Either the mule smelled the snake or felt it moving, but it would snort and jump and really caused Gill's shirt tails to pop. When we got to camp I skinned the snake and found that there really wasn't a great deal of meat on it. There was sort of a cord down its back with a strip of meat between the cord and its ribs. I cut it in about 4 inch lengths and fried it to what Gill called a "Queen's brown" and it looked really good. We fixed up a good supper, and everyone took a hunk of it. But one of the boys looked at it awhile and watched while the rest of us tasted it. None of us had ever tasted rattlesnake before, and it was really good until you got to thinking about what you were eating. Gill finally asked the kid if he wasn't going to eat his rattlesnake.

"Fellows, I hate snakes of any kind. I wouldn't handle snakes the way Ed does for any amount of money, and I can think of a million things I would rather eat than this damn snake."

But he did eat about half of his serving. It doesn't take guts to do something you like or aren't afraid of, even if its distasteful or dangerous. But when you do something that goes against your feelings or that you are afraid of, that takes guts, and that young fellow sure won all our respect. I never ate another snake, and wouldn't go out of my way to do so; but I wouldn't go hungry to avoid eating another one.

I finished up that season with the forest service and watched the boys fly out. The next job was to take the stock back to winter range down below Slate Creek on the Main Salmon. Gill, Skuke, Dan and I made the trip, and all went well until we got below French Creek, where some nut had burned the approach to the bridge crossing the Main Salmon. Gill didn't want to swim over 100 head of stock. Dan told Gill he was in charge, and they argued back and forth until they finally asked me.

I said, "Its over thirty miles around; let's swim it."

But still neither Gill nor Dan would make the decision, and they finally told me to lead out, that we would go around. I led, Gill and Skuke rode drag, and Dan had to go clear back to McCall in the pickup. We were all unhappy about having to go so many miles out of our way. We finally got to a spot across the river from Riggins. That was a trail to remember — a lot of it was solid rock, and it was so narrow that you rubbed your chaps on the rocks on one side, and looked down fifty feet in to the big, swiftly running river on the other. The trail sloped toward the river, and parts of it were wet and slippery. One mule went over, but she dropped unharmed into deep water, swam to where the trail came down close to the water, climbed out and got back in line.

A little below Riggins we came down off a section of trail that was so steep we couldn't have gone back up if we'd wanted to. We finally got to the highway, and we met Dan waiting for us by a steel bridge. We were to camp at the rodeo grounds that night, but to get there we would have to take the whole bunch right through town. Dan said he would stop traffic for us, and then direct me to where I was to cross the Little Salmon River. Going through town had to be done fast. I was to hold back the leaders, while Gill and Skuke crowded the drag, to keep them bunched so they wouldn't scatter all over town. By the time we got through town the whole bunch was at a gallop, and I saw Dan with the pickup across the highway, with traffic backed up behind, and he was pointing to a big trail on the left and across the Little Salmon. Of course I had to act fast. At the river's edge the trail forked — one went down the river, the other went straight across. I noticed that the water was slow, more like a pond than a river, and with the stock behind me at a run I didn't have too much time to decide which fork to take, so I hit the water. My horse went clear under, then swam some fifty feet across and climbed out, and of course the other stock followed right behind me. I rode up to some timber and got off, as the loose stock couldn't go anywhere but straight on to the rodeo grounds. I sat down on a log and pulled off my boots and was pouring water out of them when Skuke and Gill rode up with grins all over their faces. They didn't even get their stirrups wet. They had taken the other fork and forded the Little Salmon where it was shallow.

Gill said, "Of all the nuts, you are it! We traveled thirty miles out of our way over dangerous trails to keep from swimming, and you hunted up the only place on the Little Salmon deep enough to swim and jump the whole bunch in!"

They never let me live that down, and they told everyone we met to watch out for me — everytime I saw deep water I'd jump my horse in.

When I got back to Big Creek I found that Carol and Joe

had sold the Pinto Dude Ranch to Gordon Ray, of the Ray Petroleum Transportation Company, and I was to wrangle dudes for him. All in all, there is a world full of worse fellows than Gordon, and he meant well, but if there ever was a dude, he was it. The ranch had twenty-two pinto horses and one palomino. That palomino just wasn't right in the head, but Gordon wanted him broken to ride. I told him the horse wasn't worth breaking, that he never would be safe and someone would get hurt on him. Some horses, like some people, just aren't all there, and they're born that way. They're not mean, necessarily, but rattle-headed, even retarded, you might say, and they go to pieces easily. I broke some other horses for Gordon and he was pleased with them, but he kept after me about that palomino, saying there was no use having him around if he wasn't broken. I told him that if he wanted him shot, I would be glad to do that. Then Gordon tried to get Larry Garner to break him, and Larry told him the same thing that I had. Gordon just couldn't understand, and he got pretty put out about it. I got to thinking about that numbskull horse, and finally decided that I would climb on him. Maybe he wouldn't be as bad as I thought, and anyway he wouldn't be a source of argument. I rode him, and he was about as I had thought — not much of a bucker, but dumb and hard to teach. Gordon caught me riding him and was really pleased.

He said, "I don't know why you fellows had it in for that horse. He's the prettiest horse in my outfit. What do you think of him now?"

"The same as I always did," I told him.

One time I was riding the palomino and Dewey and another fellow were working on the trail that I was on. When they saw me coming they got off the trail above the horse, which was wrong; they should have gone below the trail. Anyway, the horse shied downwards off the trail, here the draw was about half-pitch, and ordinarily no horse could have kept his feet. I let him go, and worked on his hips with my heavy quirt and he went down and across. If he hadn't been sure footed and the ground hadn't been soft, we would probably both have been killed, but luck was with us.

Gordon asked if I thought he could ride the palomino,

Waterfall Creek entering Big Creek. Note trail bridge.

and I said, yes — as long as everything was okay, but the horse would kill him if anything happened in a bad place. He rode him and had no trouble for a few years. Then one day someone else was riding him and he bucked off in a bad place and crippled the rider for life. Then they took him out and shot him, which should have been done before he was ever broken.

CHAPTER 11

Cougar Hunting

Gordon wanted to know what we could do to get some cougar, and I told him that first of all we needed hounds. The next time he flew out, he came back with two female pups. I preferred females, because they aren't so much trouble, especially fighting each other. I named them Rip and Tear. They were crossbred Redbone and Black and Tans. I borrowed George's old hound, Dixie, which I had hunted with before. Then I caught some lynx cats for the pups to practice with. You can use house cats and hounds will learn to chase cougar, but I like lynx because they can lick a big pup, and the pups soon learn to bay them rather than fighting them. A hound that ties into a cougar doesn't live too long. The two pups developed fast, and I was about ready to take them and Dixie after cougar when Gordon flew in with the sire of the pups. Red was a Redbone hound and proved to be one of the best tree dogs I ever worked with, but he wasn't much of a trail dog.

I went up Cave Creek with Dixie, Red, Rip and Tear. We came to a bench where there were fresh elk track, which were partly blotting out fresh cougar tracks. The hounds were making a lot of noise, and I thought it was the hot elk scent in the air. I tied the old dogs up, took the pups and started to work out the cougar tracks. About a hundred feet from the bench the pups opened up and I knew we were awfully close to the cougar, so I let the pups go. Then I turned the old hounds loose, and they followed the pups to where they had treed. There was a small basin across Cave Creek, and I ran down there and found cougar beds. Two big cats had been lying there in plain sight of the hounds, and here I had been trying to shut them up because I thought they were excited over elk scent! The pups had treed a yellow female cougar, and Red was trying to tear the tree down, biting it until his mouth bled, then backing off and running at the tree. He could run, jump and cling to the side of the tree, then jump on from his clinging position and fall back like no other dog I ever saw. I knew the other cougar was close, as it hadn't had time to get out of the little basin. I shot the female and went to find the other one. There was a dead tree leaning into a green one, with brush underneath. I had gotten ahead of the dogs, as Dixie was still working on the female I had shot, and Red was hanging back listening to the others. I was just above the leaning tree when out jumped the cougar! He climbed a short way up the leaning tree, and I slapped on the tree to make him go further up, as I wanted the pups to be in on the kill for the experience. The cat's tail was just even with my face, and here came Red; he jumped to grab at the tail but missed and fell back. It was fortunate that he missed, otherwise we might have had a scared cougar right in our laps. I called the other dogs and shot the cat.

Another time I was after a cougar on McCalley Creek. I followed it up the high ridge between McCalley and Chamberlain Creeks, and at the top of the ridge under a yellow pine was a cougar bed. That cat had rolled around all over the snow on a space fifty feet in diameter, then loped off over and down the Chamberlain side, plowing a deep furrow down the hill. The dogs wanted to go, but I made them stay back. I snapped a rope onto Red's collar, as he was hard to control. The weather was cold — way below zero. The cat had gone down to Chamberlain Creek and tried to find a place to cross. I guess it was too cold for it to go in the water, so it went upstream then back toward the ridge again. I let the hounds go; they sighted the cat and followed it over the next ridge and down, where it treed. I followed as fast as I could in the deep snow, and I came upon a mountain goat which had jumped up on a rock to get out of the way when the cat and hounds went by. I wanted a picture of it, but it was in the shade, so I roped it with the cargo rope I always carried around my waist. I jerked it off the rock, tied it to a tree and took its picture, then turned it loose. (I still have the picture.) Then I hurried down to where the hounds were still baying "treed," though without much enthusiasm.

Mountain goat James lassoed for picture-taking . . . then released

I found the pups close together trying to keep warm. Dixie wasn't bawling, but Red was up on a slippery, snow covered rock bawling and whining by turns. There was a rather sharp, snow covered ridge of rock, with skidded cougar tracks on either side of the rock, then there was a big rock, and about fourteen feet beyond, a sheer bluff with a eight-inch diameter fir tree growing out of the face of the bluff. The tree was a scraggly, undernourished little thing with one fork and very little foliage. In the fork was a dark colored two-year-old male cougar, paying no attention to any of the dogs. Below him was a straight drop of about 200 feet, then a steep rock slide covered with snow that went down into the timber and out of sight. I had a .22 Special handgun that I had borrowed. I tied Red up, for I knew he would try to get to the cat as soon as I shot, and kill himself in the fall.

I straddled the first sharp rock, then scooted out to the big one, about fourteen feet from the cat in that scrub tree. I laid the gun across the rock and held it with both hands, as it was mighty cold, and shot the cat between the eyes. His head dropped and he started to slip. Then he shook his head and hung onto the tree. I shot again, and he only spit and hung on tighter. I shot a third time, and I was beginning to get uneasy, as there was only one way out of there for that cat — that was to use me as a bridge, and I wasn't hankering for that! I was satisfied that he wasn't going to drop the 200 feet down so I decided to shoot him in the lungs, as that wouldn't make him so mad and so liable to cross over me. If I could get a couple of shots in his lungs he would soon weaken from loss of blood and fall out of there. I pumped two shots into him, and decided to try my last shot in his ear and then get out of there before I got so cold I couldn't crawl back to the dogs. I made a good shot, down went his head and he started to slide, but his hips caught in the crotch of that fork. I was up against it, but I needed that $50 bounty, so I climbed over that big rock and stepped down onto one limb of the little tree. The cougar was about seventy-five pounds of loose meat and bone wedged in that crotch. I hung onto the heaviest branch of the fork and tried to slide the cat out. The tree was swaying with the weight of the two of us, and I just don't like high places anyway. I don't hesitate to say I was plumb scared. It looked to me like the bluff was swaying instead of the tree, and I didn't know how solidly that tree was anchored. One thing in my favor was that the cat was warm and I was sure cold. I finally worked it loose, and down it dropped, hit the shellrock and slid down out of sight. I untied Red and worked my way down to the slide. Old Dixie let out a bawl when she spotted the cat, grabbed at it once, then whimpered and lay down against it to get warm. Red looked at it, turned around and curled up with the pups.

It was getting late so I had to work fast. I got it skinned out by holding my bare hands on the warm flesh, then I'd skin some more until my hands got too cold. I didn't dare try to skin with my mittens on, for they would have gotten damp and frozen to my hands. I finished up, threw a couple of hunks of cougar meat to the dogs, then headed for camp, which was at the mouth of McCalley Creek. I went down Chamberlain Creek and found an ice bridge, where a forked windfallen tree lay across the creek. I got to camp just as it was getting dark and hard to see. I soon had a fire going, as a back country native always leaves enough firewood dry in his tent to last one night. I made some boiled tea and bannocks, fried some elk steak and then got into bed.

When the pups were a little over a year old, I sent Red back to his owner, gave Dixie back to George and went out after a cougar with just the pups. Up Cave Creek I found a half eaten elk that had been killed by a cougar. The cat had scented us and run. The pups bolted and within ten minutes I heard them baying "treed." I hurried after them as fast as I could, but the snow was about three feet deep, with a crust that I kept breaking through — the worst kind of traveling. The pups suddenly quit baying and came back to me. If they had been with an older hound I would have destroyed them both for coming back that way. Hounds must stay at the tree and bay. I sent them back, and they bayed a big snag about thirty feet high. I could see where the cougar had jumped and gone on. I started the pups again, and they climbed a side hill, up through a thicket of second growth firs. The snow was softer there and I could pull myself up through the thickets. The pups went out of sight to my right, quit baying a moment, then came back on my left, in full cry. Then I saw the cougar running in great bounds, and it turned up an open ridge. I hurried as best I could, but out in the open again the snow was crusted and tough going. I heard the pups baying "treed" again, and when I got to the ridge top I could see the cougar and the dogs about a hundred yards ahead of me on a steep hillside. There sat the cat, looking at the dogs — one dog on each side of the tree, really telling the world in general all about it, and that cat in particular.

The tree, no doubt, had been bent down in heavy snow when it was young, as it was almost level for about twelve feet, then grew straight up again. The pups were in the snow under the cat, and the downhill slope was so steep the bend of the tree was about twelve feet above the pups. The cat just sat there with the end of its tail twitching back and forth; the pups didn't seem to worry her much, but when she saw me she stood up and snarled and began to lash herself with her tail. I had a .22 Hornet rifle, and I had put a wooden plug in the barrel to keep the snow out, and it had frozen to the barrel. As I moved up the hill toward the cat, I was trying to get that plug out, but I had to be careful not to break it off. I couldn't budge it, so I took my hunting knife and tried to pry it loose. The cougar kept getting madder and madder. She had the whole country to get away in, but she didn't want to get away. I have come in contact with two cougar of that disposition. With most cats, you can get right up where the limb won't hold them, then they will turn and jump away; but don't make a mistake and try it with that rare exceptional cat — they do exist. This cat crouched and crept closer to me until she was at the butt of the tree, then out onto the snow. The crust held her, but I kept breaking through. All this time I was trying to get that plug out of the gun barrel. The dogs got braver and went up closer to her, and that slowed her up. But as I backed away, she crawled nearer. I finally tried to pull the plug with my teeth (false teeth) and broke a tooth off. I must have thawed it a little, for just as the cat was bracing her feet under her like a housecat ready to spring at a bird, the plug came out, and I didn't waste any time putting a bullet between her eyes!

I sent my upper plate out to a dentist in McCall, and he replaced the broken tooth with one several shades darker than the rest, and it was a front tooth. It sure was a poor job. I would like to see him and tell him about it, but I suppose he is under the sod by now. I never saw him and have forgotten his name, but it cost me $35, and I begrudge him every cent of it.

I had a big male cougar turn on me once, but I backed away and he didn't jump. I wasn't at a disadvantage that time, and shot him easily. Wilbur Wilds once got tangled up with a mean cat. His gun froze up and he was bitten four times and considerably clawed up before one of his dogs grabbed the cougar and gave Wilbur a chance to get his knife and kill the cat. The last I knew, Wilbur was still back in that country working for the government, tranquilizing

Ed and cougar. Note plate under paw for comparison.

cougar and tagging them for study. But the game has had too much expert management, and is almost a thing of the past now.

I have been back there several times, but the last few times it was like going home with no one left to greet you, and no wild life to see. I will never go back again.

CHAPTER 12

Dude Wrangling and Elk Hunting

I came in one evening (I was married to Dewey's daughter) and the Mrs. said, "Gordon left word for you to select a horse for a fisherman dude; he has a lot of equipment, so it has to be a gentle horse."

I was worked to a frazzle and I said it would just have to wait until morning. She told me that old Rex was close by, at the salt stump. Rex was a dead-head; a big powerful black and white pinto so lazy that we seldom used him except for kids. He was so dead-headed that he didn't even run with the other horses.

I said, "He is just the thing!"

I saddled him up and got on, and he humped up and walked off stiff-legged. I was tired and didn't like him anyway, so I gave him a belt with my reins. He came undone and so did I. I just sort of hovered over the top of him for three jumps, then he piled me all over the landscape. I got off my neck and turned to see what the Mrs. had to say. It was plenty.

"I knew I was going to part company with him the first jump," I said sheepishly.

"You don't have to tell me that," she said. "To think of all the mean horses that you have been riding and you let a thing like that unload you! I'm going to tell Dad."

She hurried back in the house and I could hear her grinding the telephone bell a long, steady ring which was the signal for everyone in the country to get on the line. I don't know what she said, but it was plenty, and I never did live it down. I put on my spurs and chaps and hung a loaded bronc quirt on the horn and climbed onto Rex's middle. It was dark by then and no one could see, but they could hear plenty!

The fisherman dude flew in the next morning, and as I

was in a hurry, he saddled up Rex himself. When he left he had junk hung all over that horse, and he rode down to Big Creek to go fishing. I had to go out with the pack string, so I didn't see the fisherman dude until I got back around two that afternoon.

He came over to me and said, "I want to thank you for giving me such a gentle horse. I didn't tighten the cinch up, and my saddle, equipment and I all turned and landed under the horse. Rex just stood there and let me get myself and my equipment out from under him. He was a little lazy, but I might have been killed if you hadn't given me such a gentle horse."

Sometimes a fellow doesn't know whether to break out under the arms or go blind! Take it from me — this dude wrangling ain't all fun.

I went outside to Grants Pass, Oregon, to visit a long standing friend, Howard Lewis. (Not to be confused with Howard Elkins.) I had some back country pictures, and Howard and his brothers got all raring to go back elk hunting.

I said, "Now is as good a time as any. I have my guide's licence and lots of time, so let's rattle our hocks back there."

We went to McCall in a pickup, then chartered a plane for Cabin Creek and the Pinto Dude Ranch. There was a storm on and we were heavily loaded. Jim Larkin was our pilot. Across Big Creek from Towhead Basin we hit a down draft and the plane just dropped straight down over the crags. Jim hit the top of the plane and cut his scalp open and it all but knocked him out. I still don't see how he kept the plane off those rocks, but pilot that he is, he did it. When we landed at Cabin Creek Jim was blood all over, and was a little dizzy when he got out of the plane.

After they patched him up, Gordon said to me, "You are just the fellow I want to see. The boys here tried to shoe Little Joe and couldn't do it."

I told Gordon, "Go jump in the lake. I'm a dude. I'm not working for you, I'm on vacation."

We went to the lodge and had a drink all around, then Gordon told me to come on and shoe that horse for him. I

Soldier Bar landing field. Planes land toward hill in the distance, and take off over edge of cliff in foreground.

asked him for the shoeing box, which he got, and I said, "The apron isn't here."

Joe Maby had made the apron out of a bull elk neck, and it was a really good job. I told Gordon if he didn't have any use for it, I sure did.

He said, "You can't have it. I've got it hanging up where the dudes like to look at it."

I said, "You'd better give it to me or I'll just swipe it when I leave."

"Damn you, Ed, you'd better not!" He said, "I want it to show to the dudes."

We dropped the subject of the apron then, as Howard was in a hurry to get an elk. His brother Floyd had to fly out the next day. I told Howard to grab his gun, and we went up Cow Creek. No one had been hunting up there for awhile, so I thought maybe we'd find some elk. About a mile up the trail I heard a bull bugle in the distance around a timbered bend, and I asked Howard if he'd heard it.

He said, "No, and I can hear better than you."

"Come on, I heard a bull."

We got around the bend to a big, open, bunch grass slope and the bull bugled again. Howard couldn't help but hear it that time — his ears just weren't trained as mine were. The bull was looking at us from the very edge of a small bench about 300 yards away. There were several cows with him. Howard took aim and fired, hitting him a little low. I shot quickly as we moved toward them, and missed, then Howard shot and down the slope came the bull, end over end. We rolled him down to better ground, gutted him out and high-tailed it to the lodge where we put Deckers on two horses. We went back, quartered the bull, packed him back to the lodge and hung him up to cool. Then we had a snort, got a good supper under our belts, and hit the feathers.

Floyd flew out the next morning with Bob Fogg and we went on hunting. Joe, Howard's other brother, wasn't in shape to go out hunting with us. He made too much noise and couldn't hit a flock of barns anyway. We all flew out a few days later with full tags.

We had been in the air about ten minutes when Howard said, "Here Ed, is that shoeing apron that you and Gordon were making such a fuss over." And he pulled it out from under his coat.

I told Howard what I thought of him, and added, "Gordon will always swear I stole it."

I still have that apron.

Another time Howard and I went hunting, and there was just enough snow to make the going rough. We got up to the head of Cave Creek to Dewey Moore's base elk camp. Old Dewey was shoeing horses in the snow, barefooted. He had cut off the end of a red-hot horseshoe to fit a smaller horse, and we were watching him and wondering how he could stand it. I had seen him wade in snow barefooted before, but to stand there and shoe horses like that was worse. All of a sudden he said that he smelled something burning, then he let out a bellow you could have heard a half a mile. (And he could yell — he was half Irish and half Commanche.) He had stepped on that hot slug, and his feet were so tough that he didn't notice it at first. By the time it burned through the callouses, it just kept on burning. Of course the dudes got a kick out of it, and none of us will ever forget it.

Howard's feet were all worn out from hunting, so I hit the back trail alone. Up on the ridge paralleling the regular trail I ran into lots of elk, but they were too far from the landing field to pack out in time to fly the next day. I kept going, and the spike bulls and cows would stand and bark at me, but there was no object in shooting. It was nearing dark when I saw a string of elk near enough to the lodge to pack them out, but a long way off for me to shoot. I am a hunter, and like close, sure shots; I don't take chances on crippling animals. Lawrence Johnson was due in in the morning to fly us out, so it was now or never if I was going to get any elk. (Lawrence was just as good as any brush pilot who ever flew in the back country, and a real friend, too. Those pilots really have to know their business.) I lay down in the snow on a little ridge and took careful aim at a bull's neck. It was really tough shooting, and I knew I would either kill or miss entirely. I fired, and the bull went end over end and slid out of sight. The other elk didn't even spook, but just kept on climbing and getting farther away. My sights took up the whole neck at that distance, so I aimed for back of the shoulder, and down went a second elk. I tried again and got a third one. I went down and cleaned them all; it was getting quite dark, and I was pushing myself. When I got to camp Howard was all ready to bed down, but I told him to stop thinking of his nest — we had hours of packing to do. We got six pack horses and a saddle horse each and hit the trail. We had flashlights to work with when we got there. (They are no good on the trail, as they blind the horses.) We quartered the elk and packed them on the horses, a quarter on each side. I decided to take a short cut which would save us a couple of miles, but put us in bad country. Howard said he couldn't see his horse's head, it was so dark. He was riding a big bay and white pinto called Nute — an awkward horse in daylight, but the best I ever saw at night. I was riding Little Joe, then just a three year old. He was a sensible colt, but a little spooky.

I knew the short cut would lead to a narrow draw between sheer bluffs, and when the trail started getting steep, I told Howard, "Stop. I think we are coming to the bluffs."

He got off and held the horses, and I felt around, found a pole to feel ahead with, and worked around like a blind man until I felt a dropoff. Then worked back until I came to the draw, then over to the drop off on the other side.

I climbed back and said to Howard, "Get on Nute and lead Little Joe. I will lead the pack horses. Keep out of the way and give Nute his head. They will slide into each other and some of them might not like it."

"This, I don't like," Howard said.

We got through without much trouble, but Howard said afterwards that he didn't think it could be done, and he would bet that he wouldn't tackle such a place if he could see it. (You can go through some pretty bad places as long as the ground is soft and the horses don't get to fighting.) We got to the lodge after two o'clock that morning, but the meat was in and hung up. We flew out early the next morning.

CHAPTER 13

A Guided Tour to
Bighorn Crags

We started out early one day from the Pinto Dude Ranch for a trip over to the Big Horn Crags. With me were Gordon, his twin brother and a couple of other dudes. We went from Cabin Creek to Big Creek. All the way to Big Horn Bridge was on a graded trail.

The first place of interest was where old Baldy Ables was killed by a bull on a feed lot where he was wintering cattle. A man named McDerrmat found Baldy dead, and he came and got me. Althaea was only three days old at the time, I remember. So I was the second person to see him dead. The authorities questioned me, also Joe Elliot, who was known to have had words with Baldy. They tried McDerrmat, mainly because he was the first one to find the body. There never was any doubt in my mind that an old bull killed him all right, but the case never was solved to the satisfaction of some, and a rumor still persists back there that there had been a dark deed done.

After the Ables place the country closes up and Big Creek becomes mostly white water. The trail goes down on the left side of Big Creek to the Big Horn Bridge before it crosses. I remember the trail used to cross Big Creek seven times in the first seven miles. The next place of interest was where Frank Lobar killed Walt Eastep. I knew them both, they were friends of mine, and no one could help liking them both. Walt was twenty-two years old when he came to the back country. For two years he was a forest ranger, then he became partners with Frank Lobar, who was an older man. Well, Walt owed Frank $75. When he asked him to pay up, Walt told Frank he would never pay him, that he would have to take it out of his hide. Frank ended up taking a .32 special and shooting Walt in the head. Then he called head-quarters and confessed, and even helped pack Walt's body out. At his trial, Frank told the attorney and the judge that he would kill them if they sent him up the river for very long. (I guess he considered it justifiable homicide.) Anyway, he only got a five-year sentence.

Then we came to the Dave Lewis place. Dave had been in that country for fifty years before I came there — he was a wonderful person, liked and respected by everyone. Years before, I had helped celebrate his eighty-sixth birthday there on his place. Johnnie and May Conyers had been there, too, and there just weren't any better people than they. Dave had gone to where all good mountain people go when we made this Big Horn Crags trip.

On down Big Creek from Dave's place and around a bend there are some flats (called "bars" in that country), that were the old wintering camps of the "Sheep-Eater Indians." (Sheep-Eater Indians were renegade outlaws from their original tribes.) There are still seventeen lodges, or wickiup holes there. They are about three feet deep now, sloughed in with dirt, though they were no doubt deeper when in use. The Indians erected their wickiups, or wigwams, around these holes. The holes were six to eight feet in diameter, and the wickiups were three or four feet larger in diameter than the holes. They built fires in the holes, and slept on the ledges around them. On the last flat, or bar, the trail branches off to Chamberlain Basin. It goes up Goat Creek, past Bobbin Springs and on to Chamberlain.

We went on down Big Creek and came to the first Indian paintings. They are still vivid and don't look old at all. After the forest service came into the country the trail crews destroyed a lot of the paintings in order to put a trail through the Big Creek Gorge — where the gorge closes in and the whole body of water crowds through. Across from the trail is a hollowed out place in the face of the gorge about six feet in diameter where the Indians painted a design — a circle with bars crossing and extending just beyond the circle. It's well preserved, and liable to stay that way. I can't imagine how the Indians ever managed to paint there.

Just before we came to Big Horn Bridge we had some trouble with the pack string. It's loose, sandy soil there, and the trail was all slid off. We had to untie all the pack stock,

Tree blazed by Sheepeater Indians years before the white man's coming to the Primitive Area.

for it was too dangerous to leave them tied together. The stock had to move fast and jump at times to keep from rolling down into Big Creek. They would sink into the loose soil up to their knees and jump up and on. All finally made it, but it was a wonder some of the dudes didn't go in — they were scared and did not give their horses their heads. I had crossed back and forth three times to make a trail for the others to follow. The loose stock did well, but the dudes thought they knew more than those back country horses, or were just too scared to realize what they were doing. But the horses all made it, in spite of the dudes.

On the other side of the bridge, on a bluff about 250 yards above us, I noticed about half a dozen mountain goats watching us. They will often do that for a long time, as long as they can see you. But go out of sight and they leave at once. I have had them watch me for hours that way, and deer will sometimes do the same thing.

About a mile and a half on down Big Creek, where it flows into the Middle Fork of the Salmon there is a swinging bridge spanning the Middle Fork. It swings on heavy cables which are imbedded in solid rock on both sides. Its a long span. It sags in the middle, sways from side to side, and it spooks me far worse than the bad trail before Big Horn Bridge. The Middle Fork Bridge is well built and strong and has cable bannisters on both sides. But it is so narrow that you have to remove the pack from your horses and carry the packs across. It is good that it is narrow, as that keeps the horses from turning around or jumping the bannisters.

Gordon asked me, "How will the horses act when they get on the bridge?"

I told him, "Some of them will walk across as though they really like it, and others will act about as I do when I cross it."

It's a long way down to a big river running white and swift, and I always wanted to get down on my hands and knees and crawl! Most of the horses were okay, but some we had to force across, and the worst was Little Joe. He just braced himself and even a butt rope wouldn't force him to get on that bridge. Then it came to me that I had taught him to come to me and put his head over my shoulder. There

was no place he could go, as there were men behind him
and the trail was narrow, so I tied his halter rope up so he
wouldn't step on it, backed onto the bridge and told him to
"come here." He raised his ears and came onto the bridge
and on up to me. Then it was my turn to get spooked, because I was afraid he would stampede and try to run over
me and I would have to take to the cable bannister, and I
just naturally did not want to do that! But that black and
white pinto seemed to lose his fear when he was close to
me, or maybe he knew that I was scared enough for both of
us. I am not giving you any wa-hi — I just don't like high
places. We crossed over with no further trouble.

Before you cross the swinging bridge, a couple of
hundred yards up the Middle Fork, there is a narrow bench
where a man called "Cherry" used to camp. Cherry had
trained to be an attorney-at-law, but he told me that people
as a whole were just plain no good — the high ones and the
low — and he and his partner decided to spend their lives
on the Middle Fork and Main Salmon. He was known as the
"Wild man of the Middle Fork," and he and his partner got
all the gold they wanted by cleaning the crevices in the
bedrock when the river was low during the fall of the year.
He told me he would show me the most productive crevices
if I would come down when the river was as low, but I
never got around to it. As far as I know he must have ended
up in the river. The last time I saw him was when he had
supper with me and my family when Althaea was a baby.

We stopped to noon on a rocky beach — you gotta feed
the dudes. I never stopped for lunch when I was alone. I
built a fire and had put on the coffee pot when I was inter-
rupted by excited yells from the dudes. I went to see what it
was all about, and those four dudes had treed a rattlesnake
in a pile of loose boulders, and they were so excited they
could hardly talk.

I told them, "Come on — let that rattler live in peace.
There are probably only about a hundred more in those
rocks."

But you could not have pried them away if you had a
crow bar. They wanted to know if I wasn't going to help
them get that snake.

"No!" I said flatly. "That snake hasn't done me any harm and besides, I want to lay down and sleep while you all catch some fish for supper."

I got the coffee brought to a boil, dumped in some cold water and set it aside to cool, and called them, but they were still after that snake. I lay down in the boulders, shoved some of the bigger ones aside, and thought I would sleep a little. I had a pretty tough week of it and thought I would catch up a bit, but no go. I just got relaxed when here came the dudes with a little rattlesnake that wasn't big enough to make good fish bait.

I asked them, "Why in hell did you kill it?"

"It's a rattlesnake and it might bite someone." They informed me.

I said wearily, "Yes, and there probably won't be anyone back here for a couple of years. I kill snakes around the lodge to protect you dudes, but here you are only killing something and doing nothing or no one any good. Go drink some coffee and catch some fish for supper and let me sleep awhile before you kick another rattler out of the rocks."

They did catch some nice redsides (cut-throat trout) and didn't disturb anymore snakes.

Up the trail a short distance, toward Hailey and Sun Valley, there is an outcropping of rock where there are some more Indian paintings that are really worth seeing. We went up there and they took a bunch of pictures, then we went back and threw the packs on and went on to the night camp. In the morning we retraced our steps for a way, past the swinging bridge about half a mile, up a mountain to the right and then hit the trail for Big Horn Crags. It was a good trail, but steep country and an open bunch grass slope. If a horse got off the trail or tripped over a halter rope, it was good-bye to your whole pack string. It was a switch back trail most of the way up, and those dudes wanted me to stop so they could take pictures. I told them they would have to take pictures on the move. They started to give me a bad time because I wouldn't stop, and they didn't let up until I got up to where I could safely stop, then I lit into them.

They started to argue, "But it's a smooth trail, not a tree or a rock in the way. . . ."

Flying over the Big Horn Crags

I said, "That's just it. There's nothing to stop the whole pack string if one of them made a misstep — that would mean ruined packs and a dead pack string."

Gordon said, "Ed, they will never have a better chance to get a clear picture of the whole pack string."

I was about fed up by this time, and I told him, "Here is the bell mare's rope. You can't learn any younger how to handle a pack string. I'll go to some outfit where there isn't a dude for a boss!"

The other dudes sided in with me, but that didn't make me feel much better. If I had let Gordon take the pack string I would never have lived it down, as us guides just don't do that. But if the other three had sided in with him, I would have made a half circle and headed for Cabin Creek and the end of that job. Gordon thought better of it, and we went on up the mountain.

That is terribly rough country with sharp crags sticking

up, but in between them the trail is not steep, and for the
most part is fairly good. We camped at Terrace Lakes early
that evening. There are three lakes right there — they look
to be man made, as they lay on three different levels only a
short distance apart, and they are all about the same size.
There are "pinto" rainbow trout in them — natural rainbows
with good sized white spots on them; I don't know the
cause, but they are apparently healthy fish, and they are just
rainbow trout when you eat them. There are other lakes up
there — Hart, Welcome and Ship Island Lakes. I know Ship
Island Lake has golden trout in it up to five pounds that
were planted there long before my time. I am told that
California is their native home, and that they don't get to be
more than one and a half pounds there. But the five-
pounders are in Ship Island and you can catch them if the
perpetual snow doesn't keep you away, and you'd better
have a guide who knows the country. You will run onto
Bighorn sheep up there, and they are not very wild. One
little fellow stood on top of a boulder and watched us from
about fifty yards — it seemed to have the hiccups; it shook
all over. I got within eighteen feet of a ewe and three yearling rams and took their picture. We measured the distance,
so I am not guessing.

The timber there is small piñon pines which grow up a
way, then grow back to the ground, none of them are taller
than fifteen feet, with very little foliage, and a big tree is no
more than eight inches in diameter. If you ever have the
opportunity, the trip is well worth your time and money.

CHAPTER 14

The Two Point Fire

I got a call from headquarters telling me to leave a man in charge of my trail crew, and to go to a fire with my pack string. Fire had broken out on Two-Point Mountain. I left Chamberlain and pulled for our permanent camp at the mouth of Hand Creek, below Hand Meadows and the Golden Hand Mine, which had been owned by Jimmie and Johnnie Hand, both long gone by then. I had known them when I first came into the country in 1916. I went down Beaver Creek, then down Big Creek, up Monumental Creek and past Horse Monument — a pillar some seventy feet high and about ten feet around with a big top on it. The forest service, in its monumental wisdom, has renamed it Monumental Monument, but for years it was known by the name given it by the Indians — Horse Monument. I crossed the waterspout wash-outs — here the country is all cut up for about a mile with cuts from ten to fifteen feet deep and up to twenty feet across. The waterspouts struck the mountain above and cut great slices out of it, washing down boulders as big as rooms, and cuttings great grooves in the cement gravel. The odd part is that its the only place where the waterspouts cut up the country so deeply and so many times in such a small place. The spouts have hit there for years in that small area and on that same mountain.

I went on and crossed Monumental Creek at the lower end of Roosevelt Lake, which had been formed by a mud, gravel and rock slide that had come down Mule Creek. When I first came into that country there were cabins around Roosevelt Lake on the eastern side and up the creek, and several floating in the lake. They are all gone now. I knew several people who were there when the slide came down. They told me that it took the slide three days to come down and dam up Monumental Creek. Up this creek is the old Dewey mine — a placer diggings that I have been told attracted more men, and women, than any other strike in history.

There was a Canadian company that was working that mine at this time, and we were to use their camp as our relay camp, as the truck road ended just above there. We were to pack on into the Two-Point fire. There were three of us packers: Skuke, George McCoy and myself. Skuke and I had well-broke stock — eight head to a string. George had ten head and all of them were more or less wild, — but not any wilder than he was. George was a real man in every sense of the word and an expert packer. The Canadians had a very nice camp and were wonderful people, but were really green as far as back country life went. They had a top cook called French. I had known him for a couple of years, and we just had to eat with them. None of us had had such a meal in a long time.

George told me, "Slow down before I have to drag you away to keep you from foundering. Not that I mind that, you can kill yourself if you want, but wait 'til we get this pack job done — I need you."

After we had taken on the royal gorge we sat around and had a couple of drinks and the Canadians got out a map and asked us all where we had come from. Skuke had come from Big Creek headquarters where he was alternate ranger; George had come from the Stonebreaker Ranch at Chamberlain and I had come from Arctic Point clear across Chamberlain and above the Main Salmon.

The Canadians were really excited and one said, "We're really in wild country here. I can't imagine how you all found your ways through all that country alone."

George said, "This is home to us."

The Canadian said, "I would not even venture out of sight of camp alone, and I wouldn't think of going off into that country without one of you bushmen with me."

That kind of set us back on our hocks, and when we went outside to look after our hardtails George said, "Did you hear what that Canadian called us?"

I told him, "Yes, and I've been called a lot of things in my time, but never a bushman."

George said, "I guess that Canadian meant well — we'd better skip it."

He picked up a half a sack of rolled barley. (We seldom fed grain to the hardtails, but we had orders to do so this trip, so we knew we were in for a tough time.) He went around back of what he called "his only gentle mule" and the mule kicked with both hind feet and knocked the barley out of his arms and it scattered all over. George grabbed up a jack pine that had been chopped down to build a hay manger and lit into that mule with it until it jumped into the manger, and being tied it tripped and fell in upside down. George got around on the other side and kept pounding on that hardtail until it got up and jumped back where it had started from. George threw what was left of the jack pine away, picked up the grain and walked past the mule, right up close to it, and bumped into its rear hocks. That mule just humped up with its tail between its legs.

We got going the next morning at daylight. Skuke and I gave George a hand until he was all packed up and circling his string. He had to keep them moving or they would get all tangled up and step on their lead ropes. Skuke and I got our cargoes on and tied down. We used the swing hitch — the old diamond hitch went out with the sawbuck saddles. All up-to-date packers then and now use the swing hitch. It's faster, easier and surer than any other. I went ahead, George gave me ten minutes before he started, then Skuke held back ten minutes before he followed. That was done in case someone had to readjust a pack or something, so we wouldn't hold up the pack string behind. When you stop a string, you get them moving again as fast as possible so they won't step over their lead ropes, get around a tree or get to fighting. We made about three miles an hour, and ten miles more or less was considered a day's travel. But on a fire we stretched their necks and moved as fast as we could without causing the packs to swing from side to side — a shifting pack will soon take the hair and then the hide off your animal, and it takes a long time to heal up. In the meantime you have a laid-up pack animal, which is against you as a packer.

Along the way I passed a new-fangled trail grader that

wouldn't work except on good ground, where it was unnecessary anyway. A couple of trips over good ground with a
pack string and you had a good trail, and in bad rocky
ground, as most of it was, the dude grader would not work.
About all it did was to spook the hardtails and cause us
trouble. Us packers were not bashful in telling them to take
their junk and get the hell out of the way. We were going
southeast, and soon crossed the Lookout Mountain trail,
then on down into Rush Creek.

Across Rush Creek on the northwest side, up on the
bluffs, there were some mountain goats grazing. I saw a
yearling on a narrow trail nipping the leaves off some mountain mahogany. Just ahead of the goat the trail went around
an outcropping and faded out completely. It was seventy-
five or eighty feet straight down into sharp rocks and some
twenty feet straight up to the top of the bluff. I figured there
was one mountain goat that was in bad trouble, as the trail
where it was feeding was only about six inches wide. I
looked back up the country and could see quite a way, and
no George in sight, so I stopped the string to watch, as it
wasn't a dangerous trail where I was then. As I watched, the
goat fed on around the outcropping and almost to the point
where the trail faded out, and I knew there wasn't room for
it to turn around. The goat stopped, looked down, then up
the face of the cliff, then stood on its hind feet, reared its
body straight up, twisted around and put its front feet back
on the trail that it had just come over. Then reached up and
nibbed on some mahogany and went on about its business.
By that time I could see George coming so I mosey'd on
down the trail to keep out of his way and came to the conclusion that I still did not know all about mountain goats,
but I was learning.

I came to where Two Point Creek runs into Rush Creek,
crossed Rush Creek and started up Two Point. Here the trail
(if you could call it that) went up right in the creek bed, with
sharp boulders and quite a volume of white-running water.
At times I couldn't see half my string, and the caboose mule
was out of sight most of the time. I felt sure we would lose
several pack animals and maybe a saddle horse with broken
legs or crippled stifles. But when there is a fire everything is

expendable whether you like it or not. They figure they are raising mules and packers all over the country, so what's the difference when there's a fire out of control? About two miles up Two Point I could get out of the creek onto dirt — which I hadn't seen any of for the last couple of hours. I wondered how many hardtails George had lost. That would be his hard luck, but he was a private packer and the government would pay him for any stock he lost. Still, no one likes to lose stock no matter who it belongs to.

I came upon a little scrubby brown bear with a black cub, and of course it spooked the pack string; they just don't like bear and hate cougar worse. I moved onto a little bench where there was an old natural lick. (They call them salt licks, but I never could taste any salt in them.) I spooked three big horn rams out of there — real trophy rams — they would run a little way then stop and look back. They probably had never seen a pack string or a man before and were not very frightened. That was really wild country at that time; some animals would spook a half mile away, others would just stand and watch you. I was glad to see the little sow and her cub walk away, as they could cause George a lot of trouble with his wild mules. He came in sight and all seemed to be well with him, so I pulled on up the hill toward Mormon Mountain, as I could see the smoke from the forest fire and wanted to get into camp and relieve the hardtails of their packs.

We had been told that feed had been dropped by plane and it was a good thing, because there was nothing there but a sharp rocky ridge with hardly enough room to tie up our stock. The other packers got in, and to my relief no one had any crippled stock. You sometimes feel like shooting them all, but when it comes to getting one hurt that is a lot different. A packer soon puts it in the past when an animal tries to bite or kick. I took up all the best ground to tie up the stock on, then we tried to find a place to put our beds down. There was no such place, so we tried to dig up the rocks. What little soil there was disappeared down crevices, so we moved the bigger rocks and filled up the spaces with smaller ones. We got some fir needles and put our tarps on top of that, and tried to find a place to put our hipbones.

We thought about stealing some hay for bedding, but the stock needed more hay than usual on the end of the pack job. As George said, after we made a few trips, we got to where we dozed on the trail, and by the time we got out of our saddles those rocks didn't feel as hard as we expected.

The next day we pulled out as soon as we could see and made it back to the Canadians' camp in the afternoon. We found that we had to guide in a bunch of Mexican National fire fighters the next day. (The fire was in a big basin surrounded by rock slides on three sides, and you couldn't have started a fire with a blow torch on the west side. There was no possible way to fight it out in the basin in all those rocks. Even if the timber had been worth anything there was no way to get it out. But that fire had to be put out — those were the orders. So they put it out by waiting around until there was nothing left to burn, but I'll bet my interest in the hot spot that wasn't what was on the final report.) Anyway, we pulled out the next day with Skuke herding the Mexican Nationals ahead of him, George went next, and I brought up the drag. Everything went okay until just up from where we pulled out of Two Point Creek. There was a patch of small lodge pole pines, and there was George and his hardtails. George was all right, only madder than a red-tailed buzzard. His hardtails were every way but standing up — there were mules down and mules on top of mules, all tangled up amongst those lodge pole pines. I was really polite to him, and asked if I could lend him a hand; but he was out of sorts.

"Get that grin off your face and help me get my pack string right side up, and hurry up about it!"

Of course I had to get the story before I'd crawl off my horse, and to prove how ungrateful some packers can be, he told me it was all my fault!

"Your scrubby brown sow bear was up on the side hill when I came along, and she let out a bawl and that was bad enough, but that damn little old black cub was down below playing in Two Point Creek, and of course it had to go to its ma because she called, and up the cub came."

"What did your pets do?" I asked, trying to keep a straight face.

He said, "They just climbed up as far as their ropes would let them go and let the cub go underneath them, and of course when they came down to earth again they landed on the steep side hill below the trail and took the rest of the string with them!"

I have had a few tangled up pack strings in my time, but that was a mess. Most of them were tangled up in their rigging and couldn't get up, but all of them were trying their best.

When we finally got them all up and strung out again I asked George, "Don't you want me to pull them on into camp for you?"

"How would you like to go to hell?" He grumbled, which shows that some packers just ain't had no fetchin' up.

There must have been over twenty of those Mexican Nationals, with one interpreter. He was a husky built fellow, but all the rest of them were wiry, active, slim-built little fellows. The interpreter said that they were not Mexicans. Down in Mexico they were called Bronco Apaches, and they hated real Mexicans as much as real Mexicans hated them. He told us that as soon as they got back to Mexico they would stay around town together a few days and spend their money, then take off to the hills, and if a lone Mexican ventured up there he was not likely to come back. The Apaches only came into town in a bunch, and that even here he did not trust them unless some of us were around. They all had knives with heavy, curved blades that fit into the handles, and when they fought they would let the blade rest over the back of their hands, take a punch at each other, just miss with their fists, but gash the other fellow's face. They showed it, as their faces and shoulders were all scarred up. He told us that they just fought that way for fun, but if they meant to kill they used stilettoes. They didn't associate with the interpreter and very seldom spoke to him, but they were always having a lot of fun amongst themselves, and they tried to talk to us "gringos" as they called us. One night one of then started singing, and he was really good.

After a short while he stopped and came over to us and asked, "No buēno?"

We answered, "Buēno, mas!"

That was all the encouragement they needed; there were several really wonderful singers, and they put on a show for us every night that we were in camp. We learned some Spanish and they some English. I knew a little Spanish which helped a lot, and we really enjoyed each others' company. But they never talked to the Mexican interpreter unless they had to, and he stayed away from them.

We put in twenty-one days on the trail, back and forth, packing supplies to that fire. The colt I was breaking just about gave out. I had ridden my cabbose mule, Tex, a couple of times — he must have been about twelve years old when I first got on him, so he wasn't much of a saddle animal. Little old Tex was a half thoroughbred mule, out of a hot blooded mare. The rest of the mules were out of big workhorse mares. The caboose mule had to be wiry and quick to get around switch-back trails, over logs and bad places. If a big mule was used for a caboose he would "set" in bad places — brace himself and break his halter, rope or rigging. There was a rigging of three-eighths-inch rope we called a "pigtail" linking the mules together in a string. It extended back on the mule's hips, up past the first iron bow of the decker and down and was braided into the upper cinch rings. It was made of three-eighths-inch rope so that it would break if the mule to which it was tied lost its footing and rolled down a mountain. This way you would not lose your hole string. But the caboose mule was tied solid — if he was big he would break your rigging all to pieces — but a little mule would be pulled and dragged through holes or around switch-backs, and he soon learned to keep up and not blunder into things like a big mule.

Riding Tex, I was making the trip back for the last load when I met the Apaches coming the other way. They began to yell to me and spooked Tex, and he jumped sideways and tried to run back to the bell mare. The Apaches stopped yelling and one of them came over and reached out to lead Tex for me. Now that is just as much of an insult as a rider can get — you are supposed to handle your own animal or else go get a job sheepherding.

I yelled, "Gracias, arriba," which means "up the hill."

They got it sudden and all of them climbed the side hill

on the run, yelling "arriba." I grabbed Tex with my spurs and he wrung his tail and went up the trail. If I had let that well-meaning Apache lead that hardtail, I never would have lived it down.

I went on up to the camp to pick up the most valuable stuff, and had orders to dig a hole, put everything in it and burn the rest. They believed in destroying everything that was left over from a fire. The tools would not burn, but the handles would. There was case after case of the finest kind of fruit, and vegetable and other canned goods, which I put in a hole, but I didn't cover up, because a bear would dig it up and scatter it all over the country. Dan Levan, the district manager, asked me if I covered it up, and I said of course not.

He said, "You didn't just go against regulations, but also orders; its good that you did forget to cover it up or we would have had a crew out all summer gathering it up. You are such a renegade! But I'm not going to give you credit for it, if an inspector found out, my tail would be in a crack. Besides its too late in the season for me to go up there anyway. I never had a packer who broke more regulations or who forced me to break regulations the way you do!"

He was a wonderful ranger — the best I ever saw or worked under. He did his job, and if you knew your job he just told you what was wanted and let you alone. I got him in a tight spot another time on the trail to Black Butte. The old trail followed a high ridge and went way out of the way. My orders were maintenance and betterment of the trail. I came to that ridge out from Black Butte, and instead of following the old trail up the ridge, I cut across and saved about two miles of rough trail that would never be used by a back country man. It also saved about three days hard and unnecessary work for the five men on the crew. Dan and the inspector, Lavell Thompson, were inspecting trail and caught up with us just as we were finishing the cut off. They rode up and got off their horses, and poor old Dan was up against it. There had been no orders to build a new trail, and he told me so.

I told him, "I know the orders. I deliberately built the

new trail — its better, shorter, took less work and saved a lot of labor and money."

Dan said, "Yes, I agree with you, but I gave you no such orders."

I knew Dan was caught between me and the inspector, and all this time Lavell had just been listening. He, of course, was over Dan in rank. Lavell had been raised on the South Fork and was a back country kid, but had gotten a college education and was one of the very few college experts I ever knew who had a lot of common sense. He saw the situation at once and knew why Dan was kind of squiriming. He came over with a serious look on his face, put his hand on my shoulder and said, "Ed, Dan is right. But when you come to anymore trails like this, use your own judgment and I'll back you up."

I really got a kick out of it, but if they had gone against me I would have told them to take their trail and shove it down the mountain.

Dan said afterwards, "Ed, I sure was up against it. You were wrong and you were right. Next time a trail inspector comes along I am going to steer clear of you and your trail!"

From the Two Point pack job I headed for Chamberlain Ranger Station. Gill McCoy, who was ranger there then, had phoned me and told me that my trail crew had pulled into Chamberlain and would wait for me there. I headed down Big Creek to Beaver Creek. It was late in the year, but hot — a good spell for fires and yellow jackets. I had picked up a colt at Big Creek to break for Dan's daughter. It was a pretty horse — a glass (or blue) eyed bay and white pinto. She called him Agate, and was very proud of him. I did not think the name suited him, so I called him Maggot, and she sure did not like that. Some girls are like that. Anyway, I started up Beaver Creek toward the camp at the mouth of Hand Creek. The trail was narrow and about a hundred feet up from the creek. I had only been on the colt a time or two, and he was giving me a little trouble and the yellow jackets were not helping. There were three times when the whole pack string was running and bucking at the same time. All I could do was try to stay ahead of them. If I tried to stop I would have lost the whole pack string, and most of them would probably have been killed. That angel who looks out for poor, dumb packers sure was hovering over me and my string or we never would have made it. I was lucky to have been packed light, or that angel couldn't have helped me or those hardtails, and Maggot wouldn't have ever been a saddle horse. That was the worst go I ever had with yellow jackets, and it was just plain luck that we didn't all go over the bluff into Beaver Creek. Of course a packer in that country always has trouble with jackets or bald hornets, but nothing as bad as Beaver Creek that fall. I was glad to get into camp — I don't know how many times I got stung, but the pack string got it worse than the colt and I. We just stirred up the jackets and made them mad and the pack string had it taken out on them.

I pulled into Chamberlain the next day without more trouble other than the string spooking at moose a couple of times. I don't know why they are so afraid of moose, they seldom gave us trouble. I have had bull elks chase off pack animals. One once ran my saddle horse off with them and put me afoot. I have hiked a good many miles with a halter in my hand looking for the old bell mare and promising myself that I would shoot her if I ever saw her again. When I did find her I was so glad that all I did was hug her neck.

But of all the so-called dangers of the back country, there was only one animal that I was afraid of, and I never got over it. When you turn your pack string loose at night, if they haven't been worked hard, you sleep in the trail between them and where you figure they will go. As long as the bell on the bell mare goes rattle-te-bang, you sleep like a bear cub, but let that bell start ringing at regular beats and you are out of there sudden. Many is the time I have headed them off in my birthday suit, only half awake, tied up the bell mare, then hobbled back to bed wondering how it was that I did not feel the rocks when I ran out. Now that bed was in the middle of a trail, and porcupines follow trails, and I was always afraid one would come along talking to itself, poke its nose in my face and I would slap it in my sleep and get my face and eyes full of quills.

I made it into Chamberlain, cargoed up my packs and started up Chamberlain Creek the following morning. A small black bull moose was trotting along the other side of the creek, and he was mad about something, and acted as though he wanted to take it out on the pack string. He tried to cross the creek, but the bank on his side was too high and the creek was deep and swift. He all but jumped into the creek several times, and I began to worry that I would have to shoot him if he got across. But a steep ridge on his side cut him off, and I sure was relieved. He probably had been licked by another bull. I know that is the way of domestic bulls — it is the one that gets licked that is the really dangerous one.

We came to Red Top Meadows and on up to Fish Creek where we left Chamberlain Creek. One of the crew, Jack Higby, was a fisherman of fisherman. He could hardly take time out to eat, he was so anxious to fish. That was okay with me — I like fresh trout out of a cold mountain stream. I knew the country, and up Fish Creek is Fish Lake; that lake is plumb chuck full of trout averaging around nine inches and they are really top grade trout. They will bite on anything, even a bare hook drawn through the water. Put on two flies and lots of times you'll catch two fish.

I had told Jack about it and he said, "Ed, I never caught you in a lie yet, and I'm not calling you a liar, but I just can't believe there is such fishing anyplace."

Jack was hanging insulators on telephone lines that day, the rest of the crew was working trail and I was bringing up the drag with the pack string. We usually quit work about four o'clock. Jack had gone on ahead, and about half past two I rode ahead and caught up with him.

I told him, "Put your climbers and the rest of your tools in the trail and I will pick them up when I come along with the crew. You go on up to the lake and start a fire and catch us a mess of fish for supper."(He always carried a line around his hat and hooks in his hat as packers usually do.)

He said, "Okay, I'll get a fire started, but I have my doubts about catching enough fish by the time you get up there."

I went back to the crew, and at quitting time we started for the lake. I put Jack's tools in the alfarcuss (large canvas box) on the bell mare on the way, and when I came into

Ed James repairing phone lines for the Forest Service near Chamberlain Ranger Station in 1951.

Flossie Lake

camp Jack had a nice fire going and was cleaning fish. I watched him a moment, then asked him if he wanted some help and how he had found the fishing.

He said, "Ed, that ain't fishing, its just a slimy mess; its disgusting. I still can't believe it, and I really don't want any more of it. I like to fish, not just take fish off of hooks." He paused and grinned at me, "And I haven't caught you in a lie yet."

If you ever go up Fish Creek from Chamberlain Creek watch for the lodge pole pines on the left side, growing out of the canyon. They grow clear up out of the canyon to above the bluff, and are so tall and slender that they bow back and forth in the middle in the wind, and are clean of foliage except for the very tops.

We worked on to Flossie Lake the next day, and along the way we saw lots of elk, quite a few blue grouse, a few ruffled grouse and many fool hens. We camped at Flossie Lake, and it was another wonderful fishing lake — not so many as in Fish Lake, but they average much bigger. The water is so clear that you can see everything in it. When you throw a fly in, nice sized trout come from all directions and the first trout there takes your fly. That is, if you don't become so excited at seeing all those trout speeding toward your hook that you jerk your fly out of the water before the fish get there. I have seen that done a few times with new fishermen. We made the loop back and camped at Chamberlain Ranger Station that night.

Gill McCoy told me that he had received a call from Dan that the Mexican interpreter with those Apaches had been killed on that grass fire. He had jumped off a rock, fallen onto rocks some ten feet below and busted his head in. The Apaches reported it, but would have no part in moving his body. Dan told me later that that cost the government many thousands of dollars. Your guess is as good as mine as to what actually happened.

Epilogue

December, 1976

Ed came out of the back country of Idaho while he was in his sixties and settled on a ranch in Grants Pass, Oregon. There he raised his "second litter of awfulsprings" as he calls his three youngest boys — Bill, Pat and Scott. He also raised some of the finest Tennessee Walking Horses in the state, and for years broke horses and doctored livestock for people in the area. Divorced some years ago, he got the last of his kids grown and then found himself alone with very little to do, at the age of eighty.

Never one to "hang and rattle" or sit idle for long, he spent much of 1976 relating his many experiences to me and helping me put this book together.

When I asked him about a conclusion, he said, "Since I'm still contaminating the atmosphere, I guess its not really ended. Of course we should fall over a bluff into a hole or get drowned and end it somehow or someplace; or maybe we should just snub it up to a snubbing post and walk off."

Instead he managed to sort of ride off into the sunset, in true western form.

He got restless and bored, and civilization was encroaching on him, so he decided to leave this rat-race and head for quieter pastures. He told me, "I think I'll put my horse's shoes on backwards so no one can tell which way I went, and make tracks out of this country."

So he sold his ranch and all of his horses, save one bright sorrel stud colt named "Playboy," and bought himself a ticket to Costa Rica, where his oldest son, Ed, Jr. lives. He doesn't plan to come back. December 1, 1976 was his departure date, and on that day my husband and I drove from Eugene to Grants Pass to pick Ed up and drive him to the airport. One of his hardest good-byes was probably the one he said to Playboy. ("The last green colt I'm going to

Ed James at 78, Grants Pass, Oregon

break.") Then he grabbed his one small suitcase and a satchel and we went to the airport. There must have been a dozen friends there to see him off. ("There sure are a lot of people glad to get rid of me," Ed joked.)

He really looked handsome that evening. (I can just hear him snort when he reads this, "Its been a long time since anyone accused me of being good-looking," he'll say.) He looked years younger than he really is, standing tall, eyes bright, eager to be off on a new adventure. He was all

The last colt Ed broke. There had never been anything on this colt's back thirty minutes before taking this picture.

slicked up, wearing a brand new Stetson — a going away gift from friends. He really looked the part of a western hero, surrounded by friends who were happy as hell for Ed, but at the same time sorry to see him go. He was all grins as he kissed and hugged all the women, girls and little kids; as he started to shake hands all around with the men, one of the guys offered to kiss him good-bye, too, and Ed told him to go to hell. Everyone got a big kick out of it, and it lightened the "good-bye blues."

As he moved off through the airport security gate, we all hurried outside to see him get on the plane. I felt an overwhelming sense of pride and respect for him as I watched him walk across the airstrip and mount the steps onto the plane with never a backward glance. It takes guts at any age to leave all the familiar things of life and strike out for an

Ed James and typical western gear

unknown country; Ed will be eighty-one this Christmas. As he disappeared inside the big jet I thought to myself, "He will have the plane broke to ride and all the stewardesses gentled and doubling both ways before he lands in Costa Rica."

We watched the plane start to taxi slowly away, then we all went inside, found a table by a window where we could watch him take off, sat down and ordered drinks. I don't think there was a dry eye in the crowd. As the big bird thundered down the runway and lifted off into the inky-black night sky, we raised our glasses toward the disappearing lights in a heart-felt toast:

"HERE'S TO ED JAMES!"